100 PEOPLE
You Never Knew Were at
BLETCHLEY PARK

SINCLAIR McKAY

SAFE**H**AVEN

First published 2021 by Safe Haven Books Ltd
12 Chinnocks Wharf
14 Narrow Street
London E14 8DJ
www.safehavenbooks.co.uk

Copyright © Sinclair McKay 2021

The moral right of Sinclair McKay to be identified as the Author
of this work has been asserted by him in accordance with the
Copyrights, Designs and Patents Act, 1988.

All Rights Reserved.
No part of this book may reproduced or utilised in any form
or by any means, electronic or mechanical, including photocopying,
recording or by any information storage and retrieval system,
without permission in writing from Safe Haven Books Ltd.

Every effort has been made to contact the copyright holders of material
in this book. Where an omission has occurred, the publisher will
gladly include acknowledgement in any future edition.

A catalogue record for this book
is available from the British Library.

ISBN 978 1 8384051 2 0

10 9 8 7 6 5 4 3 2 1

Typeset in Fournier and Gill Sans by SX Composing DTP, Rayleigh, Essex
Printed and bound in the UK by Clays Ltd, Elcograf, S. p. A.

Contents

Introduction 1

High Society 7
The Chess Players 23
Computer Pioneers and Technology Boffins 35
Musicians 53
The Gifted Americans 65
Mathematicians and Philosophers 75
Men and Women Of Letters 93
Polymaths and Entrepreneurs 111
The Naturalists 125
Fortunes Far Afield 133
Historians and Archaeologists 143
Journalists and Broadcasters 171
Lifelong Codebreakers 179
The Jewish Experience 197
Teachers 207
Politics and The Diplomatic World 217
Mavericks, Renegades and 'Quiet Lives' 229

Index 247

Introduction

Great minds *don't* think alike. Brilliance comes in an infinite variety of forms. The stereotype of wartime boffins, for instance, is that of owlish, awkward eccentrics in tweed, their heads filled with astounding equations and barely comprehensible calculations. In fairness, there were a few who in real life perfectly matched that description. But in 1939, as ever-increasing numbers of budding cryptanalysts started reporting for wartime duty at a country house in north Buckinghamshire, it was also the case that lightning flashes of free-associating genius could also be found among musicians and choristers, among society debutantes and novelists, among young women whose usual line of expertise was romantic poetry, even among young men who were obsessed with Highland dancing.

The townsfolk of Bletchley, a small town on a busy railway junction, the chief industry of which was brick-making, looked on in some bewilderment as hundreds, and then thousands, of these people in civilian clothes arrived at the estate gates of Bletchley Park, a Victorian mansion situated amid attractive parkland, and found billets in the rural villages dotted nearby. Equally, these new arrivals were frequently dazed by the new, intense, secret world they were plunged into. In the previous war codebreaking had been the realm of a small department of classicists, accustomed to analysing the mysteries of ancient texts. Now it was the much vaster domain of mathematicians, and a good many undergraduates in that field were pulled from university into this new challenge. But this was not the only sort of intelligence and mental strength required. Other recruits had other valuable talents and qualities.

For the codebreaking operation to be completely effective, for instance, it also required young people to run vast numbers of cross-referenced file indexes, often on shifts that dragged through the early hours. The focus and the concentration and the dedication required for this grindingly tedious – yet wholly vital – task could be found in a remarkable cohort of young women more used to glamorous cocktails and country weekends. The operation also needed brilliant linguists – supple in German, French, Italian, plus Japanese – who could work at quicksilver pace, burrowing into the layers of decrypted messages to unveil their true meaning. The young soldiers and officers, pulled away from the field, who were deemed suitable to learn working Japanese in six months had their own kind of intellectual agility.

Then there were the thousands of Wrens, many of them teenagers, whose jobs involved tending to futuristic machinery, again often through the darkness of the night. Some were sent sailing right the way across the world to work in bamboo outstations on Far Eastern codes. They had the mental fortitude and sharp wits, frequently honed on cryptic crosswords, that gave them the resilience to face complex mechanical as well as code-related problems.

In a wider sense, the history of the extraordinary codebreaking factory at Bletchley Park, and the repercussive impact it had upon the course of the war, is beguiling for several important reasons. The German Enigma codes, generated by small, portable machines a little like typewriters, were considered impossible to break. Over 178 million potential combinations of scrambled letters – and with the code keys reset every single day – presented a mathematical challenge surely no mind could surmount. Yet, with the invaluable

Introduction

head start of a trio of Polish mathematicians who had formulated methods to tackle this conundrum by hand, the codebreakers of Bletchley did just that, and very soon on an industrial basis, having invented machines that could speed their way through potential combinations (though supple human minds were still required to then crack the codes and divine the meanings of messages). The top-secret triumph of cracking Enigma gave Churchill and the War Office invaluable daily intelligence about the thoughts and intentions of the Nazi enemy, and by doing so was reckoned to have shortened the war by some two years and – potentially – saved hundreds of thousands of lives.

Another reason the story of Bletchley Park fascinates is that it is where the computer age dawned. In amid this triumph of human intellect – young, fizzing minds studying apparent gibberish and at last seeing the patterns and recursions that enabled them to unravel the codes – the Park also saw dazzling technological innovation. Later in the war, the Colossus machines, formulated to deal with the new electronically generated Lorenz codes, were among the first programmable computers. That Wrens sometimes used them to dry their underwear on during night shifts was neither here nor there. Developments such as these at the Park were to subsequently change the entire world.

But the final reason why Bletchley Park continues to exert such a hold on the popular imagination is the lives of the codebreakers themselves. Who were these people – young and old, women and men – who performed these intellectual miracles? What was it like to work under unfathomable pressure? How did they cope with these life-and-death races against time to crack codes during the Battle of Britain and the Battle of the Atlantic? What happened when they (very frequently) fell in love with one another? How did they manage to keep their work secret from family and friends?

And, crucially, what became of this astounding community of people after the war? During the conflict, some 10,000 people worked in and around the Park. They were sworn to secrecy *for life*. So how did these extraordinary minds fare in the life that came after – and how far was the unique work they did at Bletchley Park in retrospect a very apposite preparation for what on the surface seemed a completely unconnected post-war career?

In some ways, the community that was gathered at Bletchley Park, from the dons to the young messengers, was a snapshot of a nation at a very particular moment in time. These were mostly young people, drawn from across the nation and a variety of backgrounds; from the absurdly posh debutantes (girls in pearls from 'good families' were, it was snobbishly thought, particularly trustworthy with official secrets) to brilliant grammar school boys from the north; from crossword-addicted young Scottish women to a north London teenage evacuee who became the Park's youngest recruit.

And among all of these, we can now see, were a profusion of different talents: they were or would subsequently become published poets; composers; acute business minds; a ballet dancer; a famous film star; a Home Secretary; landscape historians, natural historians, a budding avant-garde female novelist, philosophers and haute fashion models.

Some of these people were to become household names; most didn't. But all who worked there were remarkable in their own ways.

After the war, not one of them was allowed to say a *word* about what they had done at Bletchley, for decades. The codebreaking triumph remained the deepest darkest official secret until as late as the 1980s. But beyond that Buckinghamshire estate, they went off after the war to get on with their lives. For a few, nothing could quite match the pure intensity of the Bletchley years. For some, it seemed to provide a rocket boost of confidence. For others, their codebreaking efforts

Introduction

at Bletchley were – in their own estimation – unsuccessful compared to what followed.

And then there were many of the Park's recruits whose subsequent lives were very quiet; they were sustained by the secret satisfied memory of what they had achieved, even if no-one else could know it. The sad thing, however, is how much of their lives they had to live – into old age, and there were those who died prematurely and would never enjoy the privilege at all – before *anyone* outside their secret community, even their spouses, their children, could know *anything* at all about what they had done in the war. 'My indomitable aunt . . . lived an ordinary life,' ran an obituary a few years ago of a woman who had just died at the age of 92 – 'or so we believed until she was able to disclose her work at Bletchley Park'.

Well-known or otherwise, a great many of Bletchley's alumni would go on to help influence the cultural, scientific, political and social landscape of Britain for decades afterwards. There will be probably less than a handful of names in this book that you will recognise for their work at Bletchley Park – but the chances are you won't be aware of the surprising hinterlands to their lives both before and after the war..

All their stories are a crucial element in the wider history of Bletchley Park, for by understanding their range and depth, their post-war passions and even their quirks, we are brought closer to seeing not only a fascinating cross-section of society engaged in a unique endeavour, but also how this collective effort surmounted the impossible. Belatedly, thanks to the lifting of secrecy and the unveiling of Bletchley Park's roll of honour, these women and men have attained a rather fine form of immortality.

Sinclair McKay
July 2021

HIGH SOCIETY

Sarah Baring

The circle of women who had seen Winston Churchill in his spectacular red silk dressing gown was rather exclusive, but the aristocratic young Sarah Norton was among them. A natural linguist, by the end of the war she had been promoted to work at the Admiralty. It was there, on one night shift, in its subterranean corridors, that she ran into the exotically dressed (and insomniac) Prime Minister.

Her life was already peppered with extraordinary encounters. In the inter-war years, finishing her education in Germany like so many other smart society girls (that it was under the Nazis did not seem to obtrude upon the lives of either the German or English upper classes, whose ritualised dances and weekends continued much as they had in the Wilhelmine era), she had been dining with a friend in a smart Munich café when Hitler and his entourage marched in. Sarah had to be restrained from hissing and hooting at him.

Subsequent encounters were rather more socially gilded and light-hearted. On VE Day night itself, she met William Astor, heir to Cliveden, son of Viscount Astor and the MP Nancy. Five days later they married; sadly, the union did not last. They divorced in 1951, her (ex) mother-in-law telling her, not unkindly, 'I think you're a goose to leave a millionaire.' Later she married Thomas Baring, a former officer with the 10th Royal Hussars and, as the Honourable Sarah Baring, continued to glide through London society with great style and humour.

High Society

Through those years, few guessed at her brilliant war work before the Churchill encounter – some of which involved *the ghastliest* social privations in a small railway town in Buckinghamshire . . .

While some who arrived at Bletchley Park were impressed with the prospect of the mansion and the lake, 19-year-old Sarah Norton found herself shuddering with distaste: it was very much less grand than some of the houses she was used to spending the weekend at. 'It was a nightmare – it was hideous,' she was to recall many years later. As a debutante, and the god-daughter of Lord Mountbatten, the elegant (and Hon.) Miss Norton existed in a realm of cocktails at Claridges, dances and hunts. She had once been photographed by Cecil Beaton.

If the Bletchley Park estate was a disappointment, the adjoining dowdy town was a shock. The Bletchley authorities were piercingly aware that while the smarter recruits would take some adjusting, the townsfolk would too, given that society beauties in fur coats were normally seen in the society pages, not in the local Woolworths. Sarah was billeted in a nearby village in what had been its 'manor house' with a 'lovely old couple', yet even this concession to gentility brought discomfort: for someone used to the luxury of central heating there was just a small two-bar electric heater. But there were compensations: an express train to London so that rare nights off could be spent in elegant Mayfair night-spots.

It was Sarah Baring's fluency in the German language (plus some 'opera Italian', as she described it) that provided her entry to Bletchley Park. At interview she exaggerated her linguistic skills slightly, partly to enhance her chances of leaving her current war work on the Slough Trading Estate helping to make aeroplanes. Given her time in Germany some vetting was necessary – 'There were a lot of young girls at that time . . . who thought that Hitler really was rather wonderful'. Not her. She was put to work updating the Park's cross-referenced card file indexes, which featured all the specialised German military terms, as well as an array of technical terms that recurred in the coded messages – a crucial resource for those charged with decrypting the daily deluge of intercepted messages.

After the war a London social life blending aristocracy and politics sometimes brought unexpected reunions with old Bletchley faces like Roy Jenkins (see page 218), though the bond could only be acknowledged with a wink.

(Margaret) Osla Benning

It is neither disrespectful nor redundant to muse on the alternative history of Prince Philip marrying the girlfriend who came before Princess Elizabeth. If he had remained with Margaret Osla Benning, he might well have emigrated with her to the wider landscapes of Canada.

As well as family connections with the dominion, this statuesque beauty had a tremendous physical affinity with the outdoors. She applied a similarly electric energy to the hard business of cross-referencing decrypted intelligence.

If other debutantes recoiled from the drearier aspects of Bletchley life, Osla Benning threw herself in with aplomb. For the canteen food, which to more refined palates seemed to consist of 'meat in water', she demonstrated an uncanny appetite, even devouring her friend's salad after a cockroach had been found in it. Another trick of hers in those rationed times was, having finished a portion of Woolton pie (in which diced vegetables made up for the total absence of meat), to slide on the disguise of sunglasses and rejoin the queue to get seconds. Her friends could not fathom how she managed to remain so slim.

Before arriving at Bletchley, Osla had been in a romance with the young Prince Philip. 'Philip who?' inquired friends. 'Philip of Greece', she replied quietly. Others slyly asked if she was going to go off to become a princess. There was a particular upper-class playfulness to their relationship, a shared love of pranks such as itching powder. But eventually it fizzled out, and Philip was soon to find his royal destiny.

Osla was born in Montreal in 1921 and had been brought to Britain when very young. She became a key figure on the aristocratic field sport circuit; to this extent, the countryside around Bletchley, which echoed to the Whaddon Hunt, had its own consolations, given that the work she and Sarah Norton did on Bletchley's card indexes was, while vital to the war effort, lethally boring. There had to be moments of escapism to counter the intensity, which further came for Osla in the form of blacked-out London nightclubs, and then a race to Euston before dawn to catch the milk train back.

After the war, she married John Henniker Major, and they had three children. She died sadly young, aged 53, from cancer. In some ways her life had been a model of discretion, both over Bletchley Park and that first romance with Prince Philip.

Dorothy Hyson

There was a good reason why Dorothy Hyson was an object of intense fascination to the codebreakers at the Park. She was one of the most notable (and notably beautiful) actresses of her generation, famous for roles both on stage and on screen. From Ben Travers farces (she was an expert light comedian, one of the most elusive of all acting skills) to crackling thrillers such as *Pink String and Sealing Wax*, her versatility meant she was in constant demand. Towards the end of the war, when theatres began to light up once more, she re-entered her natural realm, transfixing audiences in *Lady Windermere's Fan* in costumes designed by Cecil Beaton.

By contrast, her stint at Bletchley brought new demands and extraordinary crepuscular hours that left her looking like a ghost, shocking her lover (and future husband) Anthony Quayle. At the time, he was in the Special Operations Executive, itself hardly a cushy wartime option, involving as it did perilous espionage throughout Europe. 'I went to visit her [at Bletchley Park],' he wrote in his memoirs, 'and found her ill and exhausted with the long night shifts.'

Born in Chicago in 1914, Hyson had been educated in England; her evolution into the perfect English theatrical grande dame was swift. After the war, as her new husband's career brought him international film stardom, Hyson found herself in the position of acting less and spending more time carefully managing his worldwide career. He was knighted; she became Lady Quayle.

And she was at the centre of London's theatrical social vortex. As for many who had found fame in the 1930s, those early achievements were rather forgotten by the louche 1970s and 1980s.

But now, thanks to the internet and a more intense public interest in all aspects of film history (the channel Talking Pictures reflects that devotion), Hyson's career is surely soon to be rediscovered, from her starring role opposite Boris Karloff in *The Ghoul* (1933) to her turn with George Formby (who tried unsuccessfully to seduce her) in 1941's *Spare A Copper*.

Princess George Galitzine

There were those who alighted upon Bletchley Park for brief periods, like butterflies. One such butterfly went on to dazzle as a 1950s supermodel, posing for Cecil Beaton among others. Jean Dawnay also became close friends with the playwright Terence Rattigan, inspiring a character in *Separate Tables*. She found 1950s television fame as a regular on the panel show *What's My Line*, and in the early 1960s, following a particularly energetic outbreak of the Twist on a smart dancefloor, she met and fell in love with a descendant of Catherine the Great: Prince George Galatzine. Thereafter her life was divided between fashion consultancies for firms such as Marks and Spencer, and charitable work.

But the extraordinary path that took her, via Bletchley, to a much-loved home in Eaton Square, Belgravia, could not have been predicted. She was born in Brighton in 1925, in rather less exalted circumstances. Her father was a chief clerk for a meat importer and her mother, rather brilliantly, was a cinema pianist. The early death of her mother saw her packed away to other relatives, and to boarding school.

And when the Second World War came, Jean Dawnay was swift to sign up for WAAF duties, claiming to be 18 when in fact she was 17. First came work at a parachute factory. But then she was pulled into a more secret unit that was providing support for the women of the Special Operations Executive: agents who were being flown into Europe for lethally dangerous espionage work. This brought Jean into the orbit of the SOE code genius Leo Marks, with whom she began to work on matters cryptological. This meant, in turn, links with and short visits to Bletchley Park. The life of discretion suited her, and her intelligence was appreciated: immediately after the war, she was posted to Berlin to work for the Allied Control Commission, amid the haunting ruins of that city.

The post-war move into modelling came by chance, a suggestion from a friend. But in that austere era, Jean Dawnay's vivacity was much admired — some compared her to Grace Kelly. And even as she became a Princess, there was that same fizzing energy to get things done.

The Dowager Lady Egremont

In an age when the role of political hostess carried considerable Establishment heft, Pamela Wyndham-Quin undertook it with apparent ease. Hers was the era of Conservative Prime Minister Harold Macmillan: a time in the early 1960s when we had still 'never had it so good' and just a little prior to the thermo-nuclear Profumo scandal.

She was the chatelaine of the exquisite Petworth House in Surrey, as a result of her marriage to John Wyndham, heir to the sixteenth-century house and its estate. After the war, there was little possibility either he or anyone else in the family could continue to afford the maintenance and safekeeping of these architectural and artistic treasures. As with so many other stately homes in those years of austerity, an arrangement was made with the National Trust. In the meantime, Lady Egremont, as she became (her husband having been raised to the peerage in the early 1960s), was close to a startlingly wide range of people: from the explorer Wilfred Thesiger to Svetlana, the daughter of Joseph Stalin, to the Dalai Lama. That parlour game of 'dream dinner party guests' was one she was able to play for real.

Perhaps her earlier incarnation – volunteering as a Wren and being sent to work at Bletchley Park – helped catalyse both her charismatic gregariousness and her taste for adventure. Born in

1925, Pamela Wyndham Quin was among the last of the smart set to be educated almost entirely by harassed governesses. Her father was a senior naval figure, and it is probably the case that part of her suitability for Bletchley lay in her poshness: there was always a predilection among the Park authorities for aristocratic young ladies who by dint of their breeding were deemed to understand about perfect discretion. As a Wren, Pamela Wyndham Quin was among those assigned to the grand barracks of Woburn Abbey; on top of this, she was shrewd enough to bag one of the guest bedrooms. However, the lack of heating throughout the house had to be borne by all.

In later years, following the death of her husband, Pamela became an redoubtable traveller (and friends with Patrick Leigh Fermor). She was drawn to Saigon, to China, to Afghanistan, among many other places, at a time when such destinations were not always friendly.

Elizabeth Suter

Among the grey ruins of post-war Britain, there was a new thirst for colour and elegance and beauty. Just before the war, Elizabeth Suter, daughter of a department store owner in Uxbridge, west London, had enrolled at the Central School of Arts and Crafts. Her love of drawing was combined with a sharp, analytical eye for structure. After the war, that eye would lead her to the most exclusive of *haute couture* fashion houses, and to two royal weddings. It would also be instrumental in cementing fashion as an art form worthy of study for its own sake. Yet Bletchley Park intervened in Elizabeth Suter's life for quite a different reason. She maintained, self-deprecatingly, that she had been recruited because she was tall.

The theory (which was hotly disputed by fellow Wren Jean Valentine who stood four foot nine in her stockinged feet) was that tall Wrens were required to reach to the drums at the top of the complex Bombe machines as they clicked and ticked their way through millions of different code combinations. Elizabeth Suter was being modest: endurance and mental fortitude and an ability to look at problems sideways counted for rather more. And her post-war career was certainly innovative.

She returned at first to the world of art, and then moved into the more rarefied circles of fashion illustrating. This role took her frequently to the Paris collections, where her sharp, structural art, which brought out a sense of the frame beneath the clothes, became greatly sought after. This led her to the fashion department of St

Martin's School of Art, where she taught. Among her students was the young Bruce Oldfield, who credited her with great influence.

Elizabeth Suter's fashion illustrations were also used in national newspapers, and she was commissioned to sketch her impressions of the 1973 wedding of Princess Anne to Captain Mark Phillips and then the blockbuster 1981 marriage of Prince Charles to Lady Diana. Incidentally, this shone a further light on the extent of her work ethic. She had received one of the ardently sought-after invitations to the wedding at St Paul's: a guest list many would have gladly assassinated someone to get on. She turned it down. She realised that for the work she had to do she would get a much better view of Diana's dress by watching on television.

Rosalind Hudson

His Royal Highness the Prince of Wales had particular reason to be grateful to one Bletchley Park veteran: Rosalind Hudson had a singular architectural talent for creating, to scale and in exquisite detail, models of beautiful houses. This gift was not some novelty of the sort that used to feature on the BBC magazine show *Nationwide* but a fine art in its own right: her models were exhibited in the Dulwich Picture Gallery and at Bath Spa. And so, upon the occasion of Charles's marriage to Diana in 1981, Rosalind Hudson presented him with a model of his own home, Highgrove. Several years later, he had several structural changes made to the house, and he commissioned her to make the necessary changes to the model as well.

That creativity, married to sharp observation, made her in many senses a natural for Bletchley Park, where she served as a Wren. As with many of her colleagues, she had been snapped up after having confessed a zeal for crosswords and anagram puzzles. She also had a talent for the piano (a curious fact of Bletchley was that it was awash with musical talent in all its departments). She was assigned to Hut 8, working alongside Hugh Alexander's team.

Though the route to Bletchley had not been quite as straightforward as it had been for others. Born in 1926, Rosalind Hudson had been brought up in the Wirral, and had attended the Liverpool School of Art, where she worked alongside Norman Thelwell (he of the immortal plump ponies and their comparably plump riders).

After the war, her Wren duties were not immediately over; she was posted to Portsmouth, where she met her husband-to-be.

With marriage came a 1950s career redolent of the aesthetics of the era: she became an expert florist under Constance Spry, and had great success arranging all the elaborate and beautiful flowers for the luxury London hotels Claridges and the Savoy. This is turn led her to becoming the personal florist for the novelist W. Somerset Maugham and his wife. In this sense, Rosalind Hudson specialised in the art of interior design, as well as (through the models), mathematically precise architecture. She was enduringly modest, and silent, about Bletchley.

THE CHESS PLAYERS

Hugh Alexander

In the grim winter of 1953, with the spume floating off the cold, green sea, the Sussex coast town of Hastings was hosting a prestigious world chess tournament. It was an occasion that would come to inspire the James Bond author Ian Fleming.

Taking part was a studiedly diffident British player called Hugh Alexander. He was pitted against Soviet grandmasters, including David Bronstein, who had crossed the Iron Curtain specially. The set-up would subsequently be echoed in *From Russia with Love*, with the Soviet agent Kronsteen sweating over the chessboard. To chess fans and the press, the battle of wits was confined to the board. To the players it was more: they knew it was a symbolic Cold War flexing of intellectual muscles.

For Hugh Alexander – as the Soviets would surely have suspected – had a hinterland that extended far beyond the chessboard. He was one of the architects of Britain's new post-war codebreaking intelligence service, GCHQ. Yet even this did not wholly occupy him. He also wrote books on chess, and a column about the game for the *Spectator*. And during the war he had been one of Bletchley Park's more raffish figures.

Conel O'Hugh Alexander was unusual among the Bletchley boffins in the sense that he was considered rather sexy. Many women at the Park confessed a fascination for him and his deep blue eyes – even if he was simply sitting at a chessboard pondering his next move. After university he had begun his career as a schoolteacher

The Chess Players

at Winchester, but he was desperate to pursue his real passion for tournament chess. When in the late 1930s he had started winning serious prizes at the board, he had caught the attention of the cryptography recruiters: a genius for chess was analogous with a talent for codes.

As the war got under way, Hugh Alexander became deputy to Alan Turing (see page 76) in Hut 8, working on the naval Enigma codes that were so crucial in the Battle of the Atlantic. While Turing's visionary insights were to help shape the post-war future of technology, they did not quite translate to the organisational skills needed to hold a hermetic codebreaking operation together. And so it was that by 1942 he was promoted sideways, and control of Hut 8 fell to Alexander. His sly good humour and ability carried him yet further: towards the end of the war, Alexander was sent out far east to the codebreaking outstation in Colombo. And even as the war ended, the hierarchy at Bletchley Park worked hard to keep a hold of him.

In that tense Hastings chess tournament of 1953, Alexander pulled off an extraordinary feat. He triumphed. The occasion was described for that weekend's *Observer* by one Edward Crankshaw — another of the young Turks at Bletchley (see page 172), of whom more later, though naturally not a hint was conveyed to the readers. In one striking passage, though — which would have been pored over by Soviet intelligence — Crankshaw wrote of the champion in full intellectual flow: 'Alexander is on wires. His whole body moves with his mind. His face lights up with delight at a successful thought. He laughs against himself when a move goes wrong for him.'

It is not difficult to imagine that same combination of hyper-intense pressure and laughter in Alexander's codebreaking work. When he at last retired in the 1970s, the Americans tried to coax him into working for them.

Stuart Milner-Barry

It was a serious matter, but in some curious way it felt a little like schoolboy audacity. Who would be the codebreaker sent to approach the door of Number 10, Downing Street — at the very height of the war in 1941 — with a letter beseeching the Prime Minister to funnel more resources into Bletchley Park? The letter had been drafted by Alan Turing, Gordon Welchman (see page 232), Hugh Alexander and another esteemed chess champion, Stuart Milner-Barry, and it was he who was selected to run this delicate errand. This was not because he was more naturally unfazed but because, as his wife later explained in a letter to *The Times*, he was slightly older and, in his own view, more dispensable.

Becoming modesty aside, it must have taken some nerve. Completely unannounced, Milner-Barry not only knocked on the black door but, after conference with the Number 10 butler, persuaded him to take the letter to Churchill urgently. The Prime Minister was stung into an immediate response: 'Action This Day!' the War Office was told: Bletchley should have what it needed.

It is a lovely evocation of a time when a request made in good faith might have been regarded as a sacking matter. But the truth was that Churchill would never have contemplated such a thing: his admiration for the codebreakers was illimitable, and Stuart Milner-Barry was one of their steadiest recruits.

Born in 1906, and educated at Trinity College, Cambridge, Milner-Barry made his first career move into stockbroking, but it

The Chess Players

was chess that held his heart. He had won his first championship as a boy, and in the late 1930s he became Chess Correspondent for *The Times*. He was thus among the first to appear on the recruitment radar for Bletchley Park.

He established himself with great vigour in Hut 6, working with his team on all coded messages related to air and army movements. His colleague William Bundy (see page 72) recalled warmly of him that while Hut 6's head and pioneer Gordon Welchman had been 'the right opening stroke', Milner-Barry 'was the man for the long windy miles and turns. Always calm and reserved', added Bundy – 'though apt occasionally to burst forth with a deep laugh – Milner-Barry had the two priceless attributes of leadership: shrewd judgement of people and situations, and the ability to impart a deep sense of common purpose.'

After the war, Milner-Barry retained his deep love of chess even as he became a particularly Doric pillar of the Establishment, rising fast within the Civil Service to become a senior Treasury secretary. Rather than retiring at the advent of Harold Wilson's white-hot technological revolution, Milner-Barry took on a new role as Ceremonial Officer, presiding over all the diplomatic delicacies of the Queen's Honours Lists.

In the late 1980s and early 1990s, as soon as it became possible for codebreakers to start lifting the heavy veil of secrecy from their work, Sir Stuart made an early contribution to the Bletchley legend by talking to the author Robert Harris, who was preparing his bestseller-to-be, *Enigma*. By so doing he helped ensure that blockbusting popular fiction and extraordinary historical fact could conjoin to create a story that fired the public imagination, and in the process do so much to save Bletchley Park itself from demolition.

Hugh Foss

At first glance – a mistaken glance – Highland dancing is rather ornamental and quaint; a shortbread-tin tradition aimed at amusing Sassenachs. But as with many innocent hobbies, there is rather more to it. Those with a keen eye who examine diagrams of the dance moves might, for instance, detect an intricate mathematical side to the pursuit.

Back in the 1950s it had a magnificent champion in the shape of Hugh Foss. He was a distinctive figure, standing six foot five with russet hair and a long beard. He was also an avid kilt wearer. And Foss went further than many with his love for such dances. He invented new ones, all immortalised in those code-like dance patterns. When there was a craze in post-war Chelsea for Highland dancing, Foss twirled at the centre of it.

Such a figure would never have been an ideal undercover agent. He was, however, a searingly good codebreaker with an extraordinary hinterland. He had been born to missionary parents in Kobe, Japan, which equipped him with one of the invaluable linguistic attributes he brought to the Bletchley operation. The deciphering of Japanese ciphers ought to have been particularly intractable, but people such as Foss, recruited to the cryptography operation back in the 1920s, found a way through.

When war came, he was put in charge of Hut 7, and colleagues had fond memories of Foss using breaks to put his feet up and solve crosswords in Russian. Nor did any of this hinder his maniacal Highland dancing; he took the old ballroom of Bletchley Park (which had a moulded ceiling 'like drooping bosoms', as Sarah Norton recalled) and, with a gramophone, encouraged young graduate codebreakers like Oliver Lawn and Sheila MacKenzie (see pages 84 and 138) into evenings of pipes and energetic swirling.

His obsession was partly the fault of his Scottish wife Alison, who in the 1920s had taken her husband along to an evening of Highland dancing and watched astonished as it seized his imagination. During daylight hours, Foss was also ahead of his time in wearing sandals with socks. Indeed, he simply refused to wear conventional shoes. When he sailed for America to share intelligence and cryptographer techniques, his amused Washington hosts referred to him as 'Lend-Lease Jesus'.

He was never underestimated, though: when the Americans and the Japanese went to war in 1941, his insights were invaluable. Back in England, evenings with the Fosses could be fraught. They were both especially particular about how washing-up should be done: always saucers first, as they had 'least contact with human lips'. One unwitting guest helpfully brought in some cups and was on the point of placing them in the bowl when the Fosses wailed, 'Oh! You mustn't do the cups yet! Saucers first!'

Like so many of his cryptographer colleagues, Hugh Foss was kept in the loop after the war, as one of the tiny number of people privy to the new GCHQ codebreaking realm. But while he was not inhabiting this hyper-secret world, he was delighting another sort of hermetic community with a new magazine – one naturally devoted to Highland dancing, with some new dances of his own design, including 'Black Craig of Dee' and 'Who'll Be King But Charlie?'

Harry Golombek

There were those whose devotion to chess made them not only great players but also great scholars. Quite aside from his buccaneering cryptological career, Harry Golombek, an International Grand Master, built up an extraordinary library devoted to chess, which led to him becoming fluent in Russian as well as German. In the 1950s he also travelled frequently to the Soviet Union to learn more about the minds of their grand masters – this at a time when shuttling back and forth across the Iron Curtain would have been viewed with suspicion in some quarters. But chess knew no borders. And Golombek's ceaselessly curious intellect was a perfect match for Bletchley Park.

Unlike some of his classicist codebreaking colleagues, Golombek, born in 1911 in London's East End, was grammar school-educated in London, and went on to London University. But like many of his Bletchley fellows he had found precocious success with chess, playing in international competitions throughout the 1930s before being snapped up for codebreaking duties. Though he had already been drafted into the army when the call came, in fact it was his own artillery officer who had alerted the relevant intelligence departments to the prodigy among his squaddies, telling them that Golombek 'had too much brains to be behind the guns'.

As well as a knife-keen intellect, Golombek also had a natural facility for languages. And he had the ideal temperament for codebreaking: when faced with the knottiest abstract problems, he had a talent for remaining relaxed and witty. Golombek later reflected that deciding to leave military training for cryptography probably saved his life: during the course of the war most of his battalion were killed.

After the war, as a 'chess-book-writing country squire' in Chalfont St Giles, he was another of the Park's chess correspondents for *The Times*; he also took the helm of the World Chess Federation. While he would have been intensely aware of all the Cold War undercurrents in these international tournaments, the game nonetheless had for him a crystalline purity and fascination. He was also regarded as a 'distinguished arbiter' in matches between Russians and Americans.

Nor were his efforts to bring the game to a wider public ignored: in 1966 he received the OBE for services to chess – the first person to receive such an honour. But at Bletchley Park he had earned an even greater distinction: at the chessboard he took on the mighty intellect of Alan Turing, and won comfortably.

Professor David Rees

While the wartime security surrounding Bletchley Park was super-tight, occasionally unexpected chinks of light revealed to the wider world that something distinctly odd was going on in this corner of Buckinghamshire. One such was a chess tournament in the early 1940s, billed as Oxford University versus Bletchley. The finest Oxford minds, local newspapers were intrigued to report, had been beaten by the intellects found in a town known mainly for the manufacture of bricks. On that winning team was a shy mathematician who had also enjoyed one of the Park's earliest codebreaking triumphs. His name was David Rees.

Born in 1918 in Abergavenny, Rees went to grammar school, and was engaged in post-graduate mathematics at Cambridge when war broke out. It was fellow Sidney Sussex alumnus Gordon Welchman who drew the 21-year-old to the Park. Details were initially sketchy. 'We want you to go to this top-secret place to carry out vital work for the war effort,' said Welchman, 'but we are not going to tell you where it is.'

'Fine,' said Rees, 'but if you are not going to tell me where it is, how am I going to find it?' Given his epic shyness, this rejoinder was startlingly bold.

Welchman had chosen well, though: in May 1940, as the German forces flooded through France, Rees worked through the night on a set of messages and was able to break into what was known as the Red cipher, after applying an ingenious method devised by his colleague John Herivel (see page 86), unlocking great swathes of them by hand. Such was his achievement that his fellow codebreakers clambered onto their desks to applaud him. He insisted the honour was not his.

Later on, Rees was among the gifted minds transferred to Professor Max Newman's department, working with the Heath Robinson and Colossus, and after the war he followed Newman (see page 39) to Manchester to be there at the inception of the computer age. But his passion was for algebra, of a variety that was particularly abstruse, and yet also revolutionary in its way (he paved the way for the solution of Fermat's Last Theorem, for instance).

Rees subsequently returned to Cambridge, and then took the chair of pure mathematics at Exeter, also serving as the university's vice chancellor. His students affectionately bestowed upon him the coveted 'Patrick Moore Look-a-Like of the Year' award. He was elected to the Royal Society as a Fellow; 40 years later, his daughter Mary was similarly elected – the first contemporaneous father and daughter Fellows. He was always discreet about Bletchley, yet his contributions in the austere Hut 6 did much to rocket-boost the morale of the establishment after its slightly uneven start.

COMPUTER PIONEERS AND TECHNOLOGY BOFFINS

Irving John Good

How might a machine come to think for itself? Might such a creation develop its own mind, its own personality, its own soul? For a time, the subject absorbed Professor Jack Good intensely. He directly inspired the author Arthur C. Clarke, who wrote *2001: A Space Odyssey*. And in 1968, he was approached by the film director Stanley Kubrick to help with his adaptation, and to give his thoughts on the chillingly murderous computer HAL in the storyline.

All this was the perfectly natural offshoot of Professor Good's younger days at Bletchley Park, where, as well as decoding messages from the very heart of the Nazi regime, he and his colleagues were setting up the framework for the forthcoming global computer revolution. Ever since childhood, Jack Good had moved at quantum speeds.

He was born Isidore Jakob Gudak in north London; his father was a watchmaker. Perhaps that mathematical delicacy and precision fired something in his young son's imagination: briefly bedridden with diptheria aged nine, young John, as he was by now known, occupied himself by fretting over the 'irrationality' of the square root of two, and devising an algebraic formula to demonstrate that the equation could have a seemingly infinite number of solutions.

This wild mathematical precocity took his teachers at the well-respected Haberdashers Aske school rather by surprise: lessons became embarrassing, as the maths masters simply could not keep up with the intense brilliance and insight of their pupil. For these periods, he was eventually sent to the library to study alone. Thankfully, his academic record was not perfect: he had been a little slow when it came to taking up reading.

Bletchley Park recruited him directly from Jesus College, Cambridge, where he was an undergraduate. In 1941 he was summoned to meet Hugh Alexander, who asked him if he might be interested in working for the 'Civil Service'. Even the unworldliest of students would by then have understood what that meant. His first posting was in Hut 8, with Alexander and Turing, at a point in the war when the bulky 'Bombe' machines were whirring through thousands of potential code combinations and it was becoming clear that there was room for a great deal more technological progress.

Good and Turing clicked immediately: their chess contests were fierce. But Turing was transferred for a time to the US, and the young Good – who specialised in a field called Bayesian statistics – moved over to the department known as 'the Newmanry', presided over by Professor Max Newman. The computer revolution was germinating within Bletchley's slabby concrete blocks.

As Nazi encoding technology had evolved – the Enigma machines were still in mass use, but the more advanced Lorenz system was now being employed by Nazi hierarchy – so too did Bletchley's response. There was an extraordinary innovation that looked so loopy and ramshackle – spindles, tapes, threads, drums, all the size of a wardrobe – that it was christened the Heath Robinson, after the vintage cartoonist of outlandish inventions. But it worked. This in turn led to the Colossus machines, which were in effect the first programmable computers. Good sensed when the machinery was about to go wrong: first, he would detect a change in noise, then the odour it was giving off.

This exploration of computing continued after the war, as Good followed Turing and Professor Newman to the University of Manchester. A variety of academic and commercial roles followed, plus a range of books of which even the titles were eye-wateringly abstruse (*The Estimation of Probabilities – Modern Bayesian Methods* was one). His secret life continued too: just several years after leaving Bletchley, he was persuaded to join its regenerated form, GCHQ. Though the facts are still very much smothered by the Official Secrets Act, that computing knowledge must have played an intriguing role in the Cold War.

Professor Max Newman

Although only 45 years old when he arrived at Bletchley Park in 1942, Professor Max Newman might have appeared more venerable next to his youthful graduate teams. Here was the man who had inspired Alan Turing: his famously clear mathematical lectures – delivered without notes – sparked the younger man into writing one of his first monographs. Like Turing, Professor Newman was fixated on the possibilities of the age to come. He came to have a section at Bletchley named after him – the Newmanry – as he and his young colleagues worked at the intricacies of the German *Sagefisch* (Fish) coding system. It was under Newman that the 'Heath Robinson' and Colossus machines came into being (as we have seen, the former so-called because of its resemblance to a mad invention drawn by the eponymous cartoonist) and he and Turing were to continue their exploration of computing possibilities at Manchester University.

The Professor was forward-looking in other ways. Initially, like many of his generation, he had been resistant to the idea that young women were every bit as able as their male counterparts to deal with technological complexity. But once he had been persuaded that this was foolish, he became a remarkably inclusive team leader, encouraging anyone and everyone – from the most intense mathematical scholars to the young Wrens with a lively taste for crosswords and whodunnits – to contribute ideas. There were regular meetings at which any idea of hierarchy was pushed aside.

Newman was born in London in 1897, in the final flickering of Victoria's age. His father had been German; the son only anglicised his own name from Neumann in 1916 because of anti-German passion during the First World War. Although immersed in academia, he married outside it: his wife Lynn Irvine was an 'accomplished' novelist, the daughter of a Church of Scotland minister. Newman could appear to some austere, but perhaps it was more a quality of gentle thoughtfulness. He was noted as an excellent pianist – one of many attributes that recommended him to the codebreaking establishment. He was also a rather wonderful writer in his field, as many of the younger codebreakers at Bletchley noted. His texts on mathematical theory – which alas would be rather too abstruse a prospect for the unschooled reader – were accounted by some to be 'limpid' and almost poetic, demonstrating 'mastery of language'. In private, he was also noted for having 'a quite delightful turn of phrase'.

Newman was also an intensely loyal friend. At Alan Turing's 1952 trial on the charge of gross indecency, Professor Newman was there to provide a vivid and moving character witness for his young protégé; at a dark time in British public life when homosexuality was the focus of a witch-hunting hysteria, it also took some courage to publicly stand shoulder to shoulder with the accused. Across the years, Professor Newman himself inspired terrific loyalty; and even after he retired from the University of Manchester, he continued to teach, this time at Warwick University, and his students were always impressed by both his scrupulous clarity and his warmth. There is the question of modesty too: for it was while at Bletchley Park, working in the concrete extensions, that the Professor was among a handful of people who were instrumental in shaping the future course of history.

Professor Bill Tutte

It was a codebreaking proposition many times more complex than even Enigma. Given the name 'Tunny', this was the system by which Hitler and the most senior Nazi personnel were communicating with the generals. The machine was the Lorenz SZ40 teleprinter, which had twelve code-generating wheels, four times as many as Enigma. Messages would be transformed into binary encryptions, fed through the machine and then transmitted through the ether, where they would be unscrambled at the other end by another Lorenz machine. Making the challenge to Bletchley Park even greater was the fact that no-one in the UK had ever caught sight of this technological marvel.

Incredibly, it was a young chemist called William Tutte, someone passionately interested in the natural world, who pulled off a feat some had considered impossible: he sat down and, using painstaking mathematical deductions and imagination, as well as pencil and paper, he conjured his vision of the Lorenz machine and its innermost workings. Applying exhilarating lateral leaps, Tutte envisaged the teeth of the code wheels, the way all the wheels moved together, regularly and irregularly, and how the codebreakers might find formulae with which to pry open the encryptions.

The image of the workings Tutte could see in his mind's eye proved amazingly accurate, and after some weeks it proved possible – if slow and cumbersome – to break the Tunny messages by hand. This was where Professor Max Newman and his 'Heath Robinson' electrical innovations came in. But Tutte remained enduringly modest about the fact that, thanks to him, it was now theoretically possible to read messages directly from Hitler's desk, sometimes before the intended recipients themselves.

Tutte's background was not obviously academic: born in 1917 and brought up near Newmarket in Suffolk, he went to the local county high school, and then on to Trinity College, Cambridge. Recruitment to Bletchley Park had come because in the late 1930s one of his former tutors had been dazzled by some of Tutte's intellectual improvisations concerning the study of electrical circuits.

The post-war years saw Tutte, like his colleagues, keep firmly quiet about his codebreaking years (and particularly the amazing and lasting contribution he had made). He was persuaded to emigrate to Canada to join the University of Toronto, and then Ontario, where he was fêted and revered. It was said that one of his greatest satisfactions was the chance to live in a super-peaceful village near the campus; a community that reminded him of his summer Suffolk youth on lazy lanes amid droning bees. Nor did he lack for hinterland: he and his wife Dorothea were fanatical walkers, and the vast open spaces of Canada gave them illimitable territory to explore. He also shared one passion with a large number of Bletchley Park's Wrens: he adored detective stories of every variety.

Tommy Flowers

Few can claim to have been honoured with their own mural. Yet at one end of a regenerated shopping parade in an otherwise down-at-heel corner of London's East End, hemmed in by feeder roads for the Blackwall Tunnel, is a magnificent portrait of a bespectacled young man. He looks a little like the 1940s comedian Arthur Askey.

In a curious way, the man in the mural also brought a lot of harmless pleasure after the war to Britain's working classes, as we shall see, with the invention of a machine called ERNIE. He also, along the way, built what was pretty much the world's first programmable computer.

His name was Tommy Flowers, and he is now revered not merely among today's cryptographers, but also amid the dazzling colonnades of Google and Apple. Tommy Flowers had a strong hand in shaping our own computer-led age. That is why his image – vast and benign – is on this Poplar wall. For in 1905 this was where he was born.

Flowers did not come into Bletchley Park's orbit through academia; rather, he had a genius for engineering. Through apprenticeships at the Woolwich Arsenal (at the other end of that Blackwall Tunnel) and through diligent studies at night school, Flowers progressed fast to join the General Post Office, which then ran Britain's telephone network.

He was based at a large research laboratory on top of Dollis Hill in north-west London, and by the onset of war his innovative work had been noted by people like Alan Turing. When Bletchley Park began using its own 'Heath Robinson' machines to chunter through the Lorenz codes, there was disappointment at how fragile and unreliable the technology was. Flowers, fully inducted into the Bletchley secret, had his own ideas for a new machine. But to the debonair Gordon Welchman he was merely 'the crafty cockney' – partly a way of looking down on his lack of Oxbridge qualifications – while his novel ideas for using valve technology met further resistance.

So he built the Colossus machine largely out of his own pocket, with whatever parts he could obtain – and succeeded beyond anyone's most lurid dream. When the Colossus was tested with a known code, the results were superlatively accurate; nor did it break down. The trick was to never switch it off. With all its glowing valves it gave off tremendous heat. At night, Wrens used to furtively dry their underwear on it. But the Colossus opened a window directly onto Hitler's desk.

Obviously, Flowers was sworn to secrecy; after the war he was awarded the MBE, but was never allowed to tell anyone what for. He was rewarded with £1,000, but could never reveal that this was simply to pay him back for his own personal expenditure when developing Colossus.

In the 1950s he did reach some level of public acclaim, though as the inventor of ERNIE, the Premium Bonds computer that every week randomly selected the number of the bond that would win a substantial cash prize. Like the football pools, ERNIE became synonymous with good-humoured daydreaming about a life of leisure. And by the 1980s, he was at last free to tell his family – as well as the wider world – what he had achieved.

Donald Michie

Here was a computing genius with the apparent gift of prophecy. In 1968, Donald Michie had a vision of what we now know as the internet. 'Along with question-answering services, which will allow us to inquire about the restaurants in our locality or politics in Paraguay,' he told the British Association, 'will come the games opponent, the puzzle setter and the quiz master'. Michie was fond of games, and he was also fond of programming machines to play those games. If Alan Turing had wondered about the metaphysical possibilities of an intelligent artificial mind having an eternal soul, Donald Michie was alive to the earthier possibilities: could we ever completely trust an artificial mind with nuclear material?

One didn't have to be a mathematical prodigy to either break codes or indeed see how the machinery in Bletchley Park might eventually evolve into thinking computers that could revolutionise the world. Donald Michie was educated as a classicist, but his years spent cracking ever-more complex encryptions inspired visions of the future that might only otherwise be shared by science fiction writers. Unlike most of them, Michie's predictions about what the new world of computers might look like were, in hindsight, genuinely uncanny. He was himself something of a Renaissance man – quite genuinely, in the sense that his intellect was free-ranging, blending science and philosophy. Yet he was known at Bletchley Park by the undignified nickname of Duckmouse.

Born in Rangoon in 1923, and educated at Rugby, then Balliol, Michie supplemented his flair for the classics by curating the 'Balliol Book of Bawdy Verse'. By the time he was pulled into Bletchley Park, codebreaking had definitively entered the machine age, although the machines still needed the raw intelligence of those feeding in the information. This decryption production line fascinated Michie, and he began to have discussions with Alan Turing, the great pioneer of Artificial Intelligence. Might a machine learn how to play chess? And if a mechanical mind could do that, what might not be beyond its capabilities?

Beyond Bletchley, Michie changed academic direction, moving into medicine and genetics, but also staying in close contact with Turing about the new generation of computers. After Turing's suicide, Michie redoubled his own momentum in this potential new field. By the late 1950s, he had developed a machine that could play noughts and crosses. His work was of interest to the Americans, but he was now a fixture at Edinburgh University, where his genetics work went side by side with computing. By 1966, he was running the Department of Machine Intelligence and Perception.

And by the 1980s he had secured a fine tribute to his old friend, when he became Emeritus Professor at the newly formed Turing Institute at Glasgow University. How would this new generation of computers be used, and whose thoughts would they think? He was also writing columns for newspapers outlining the possible hazards of this new sort of intelligence. 'Is there a danger,' he wrote in the *Observer* in 1989, 'that the brute-force calculating power of the computer will soon transcend the grasp of the human mind?' Quoting the chess master Gary Kasparov's comment that computers 'have their psychology too,' Michie mused, 'That may be so. But is it the kind of mentality that we want in charge of a nuclear power station?'

Professor Michie's career was confirmation that, as well as helping to shorten the war by two years, Bletchley Park had been one of the world's most creative hothouses. Given the draining nature of the work and the pressures of time, young people like Donald Michie had been able to look about themselves with wonder at what was being achieved, and at how much more might be achieved when peace had come once more.

Arnold Lynch

The scientific advances that the codebreaking operation catalysed placed Bletchley Park at a sort of technological junction point: it relied on a blend of analogue mechanical genius and super-futuristic electronics that pointed the way to the future. While Tommy Flowers, with his Colossus machine, was pre-eminent in making that future practicable for the Park, he was not alone; there was also a marvellous engineer/scientist called Arnold Lynch based in those north-west London laboratories on top of Dollis Hill.

Like Flowers, Lynch came from an unprivileged London background; also as with Flowers, his was a life of ceaseless scientific work and curiosity. In some senses, Lynch was the man who actually made Colossus possible: he was a pioneer with photo-cell technology, giving electric machines the ability to 'read' via optical tape. In time, his work went a long way towards making advances like miniature radios possible. In many ways he was the model Bletchley boffin: his work was all-consuming, his enthusiasm illimitable.

Lynch was born in Tottenham in 1914, when that area of North London was highly industrialised; his father was a local headmaster, and he himself had a natural academic streak, winning a scholarship to a school in Islington and then Emmanuel College, Cambridge. By the mid-1930s, the young man was mesmerised by leaps in technology and, although it sounds strange now, one of the centres of electronic experimentation was the General Post Office, largely due to wireless and the ever-growing international telephone network falling within its remit. The laboratories in that cheerfully grand building at the summit of Dollis Hill were festooned with wires and valves and flashing lights. To get a position there was not easy. Lynch sat an examination with a great many others. But once in, he was the ideal recruit.

And come the war, the relationship between Bletchley Park and Dollis Hill was sealed. The technological achievement of Colossus meant the codebreakers could open a window into the secret messages of the Nazi hierarchy; Lynch's breakthrough with optical tape readers meant Tommy Flowers' creation could also work at hitherto unimagined speeds.

The post-war world meant, for Lynch, an entirely new realm of electronic possibilities. He and Flowers could see new applications for their work everywhere. Lynch stayed at Dollis Hill until 1974, when retirement loomed, yet he never stopped working. Fresh avenues of electronic research were explored, at City University and University College London. He also took up a position at the National Physical Laboratory in south-west London to look into advances in electrical engineering – following in the footsteps of Alan Turing, who had spent some time at this important institution in the 1950s.

Gil Hayward

At heart, Gil Hayward was an ingenious inventor who would have been a perfect 'Q' for Ian Fleming's James Bond. Long before the first of those novels appeared, Gil Hayward was ahead of the game when it came to espionage gadgetry and innovative, fast-moving vehicles. It was his ingenuity, together with that of Tommy Flowers, that enabled the codebreakers to read Tunny messages emanating from German High Command and from Adolf Hitler himself. Hayward was the electronics expert who made the progression towards the Colossus possible. Rather in the manner of Tommy Flowers, that ingenuity went still further beyond the war, extending to gyrocopters, harpoon guns and hovercraft.

Hayward was born in 1917 in the London suburb of Kilburn, and the early signs of his inventiveness were there when as a boy he built his own telescope. There was not the money to contemplate university, but there was the consolation of an apprenticeship at the Dollis Hill laboratories which would become so interlaced with Bletchley throughout the war years. However, Hayward's war saw him move off at an angle: he was sent to Egypt with the Intelligence Corps, and it was there he honed the fine science of bugging.

Nineteen forty-four was the year that saw him brought back and enfolded within Bletchley's endeavours, creating replicas of German Tunny machines. He was still a captain as he served in the department known as 'the Testery' (after Ralph Tester), wrangling complex electrical systems.

Nor did victory staunch the flow of his ideas. After the war, he worked on voice encoding systems. But he was also one of the last men of Empire: he had a spell in the Far East with the intelligence unit of the Royal Malaysian Police, devising means by which to quell the insurgency. He also had a spell in Ghana working on telecommunications (this is where his home-made hovercraft made its appearance).

His technological legacy is found criss-crossing the world's oceans today: electronic encrypted seals for containers of goods being shipped to all continents. Hayward was also invaluable in securing Bletchley's legacy: strictly against regulations, he had kept the super-classified blueprints for Colossus, enabling the machine to be rebuilt decades later.

MUSICIANS

James Bernard

Anyone who has ever seen one of the gaudy Hammer Horror films from the 1960s has heard James Bernard's extraordinary and atmospheric music: swirling neurotic strings and heartbeat percussion as Dracula pursues various nightgowned women through the trees at the back of Pinewood. What is much less well-known is that this prolific composer had been a Bletchley Park codebreaker. Yet there was always a curiously strong musicality running through the Bletchley story.

Bernard was born in a hill station in India in 1925 and went to boarding school in England, where he excelled at piano. Joining the RAF in 1943, he was very soon talent-spotted for cryptography work, and sent to the Japanese section. This was a time in the Park's history when distinguished classical performers such as Myra Hess and Peter Pears were being invited to give concerts there – having no idea for whom they were performing. It was Gordon Welchman who had noted that curious affinity between musical composition and cryptographic ability.

After the war, Bernard studied at the Royal College of Music, began composing for radio, and fell into Hammer's house of horror almost by accident when another composer, John Hollingsworth, was too ill to complete a score for a Quatermass film. In the subsequent chillers, Bernard employed the musical motif of the augmented fourth – associated in medieval times with the Devil and, as a result, banned until the sixteenth century. Away from the Gothic hokum,

Bernard lived with the writer and poet Paul Dehn (who wrote the script for *Goldfinger*), and they won an Oscar for the original screenplay for the thriller *Seven Days To Noon* (1950). In addition to all this, Bernard was a valued friend of the composer Benjamin Britten and assisted him with the score of the opera *Billy Budd*.

It might seem odd nowadays that such an intelligent and creative composer in his own right should be remembered chiefly for films such as *Kiss of the Vampire*, but Bernard was always proud of his work, citing influences such as Debussy and Liszt. He died in Jamaica in the year 2000, and it is instructive now to think of Bernard employing that instinctive musician's talent – the ability to hear notes that aren't there – to bring meaning to the dissonant chaos of encryptions.

Brinly Newton-John

Any father might be delighted and proud that his daughter's global pop music fame almost entirely eclipsed his own career. But Professor Newton-John, father of Olivia, had the satisfaction of a range of secret achievements. Not only was his time at Bletchley Park marked by some crucial work that contributed towards the defeat of Rommel, but he was also a key figure in enriching the Park's cultural life, giving the codebreakers much-needed escape from terrible pressure.

Born in Cardiff in 1914, Newton-John went to Cambridge, where he studied languages. He had a fascination for Germany: not just its literature, but all aspects of its culture. His first career move was that Evelyn Waugh-ish standby of schoolmaster at minor public schools. His first marriage was rather more striking: his bride Irene Born was the daughter of the famed German physicist Max Born.

The war saw Newton-John drafted first into RAF intelligence where, among other remarkable assignments, in 1941 he was among those to interrogate Rudolf Hess. He was also involved in questioning other German airmen shot down over Britain. Meanwhile his immersive knowledge of all the subtleties of the German language, plus his intellect, saw him picked out in 1942 for Bletchley.

It was in part his codebreaking work in Hut 3 which revealed the sorry state of Rommel's supply lines. But it was also his alertness to the nuances of the German class system, and the linguistic tics thereof, that enabled him to interpret other decrypts. Later, he was pulled into the effort against the Japanese codes.

Meanwhile, when off duty, he took to the Bletchley stage; surviving revue programmes bear his name. But he was not merely there for light entertainment – Newton John was a passionate opera singer, and gave renditions of German *lieder*: a strikingly counter-intuitive choice in the depths of war, but indicative of a belief that German culture far transcended the common criminality of Nazism.

The post-war years brought more teaching, and a move to Australia to join the University of New South Wales, where he rose to become vice-principal and emeritus Professor of German. Always a popular teacher, Newton-John remained true to his musical passions too, presenting classical music shows on radio and lecturing on the great composers. As his daughter Olivia was storming the world in the 1978 hit film *Grease*, Newton-John was enlightening his listeners on the beauties of Bach, his expertise giving him a presence on Australian television as well.

Then the Bletchley secrecy began to lift and he was able – with some care – to talk a little about his war years. His daughter Olivia, meanwhile, wrote beautifully of the power of music over her parents – and of how it brought them together. 'One day,' she wrote of her mother, 'she heard a man singing in a deep baritone voice and she couldn't take another step': she 'fell in love with the voice first before she even saw him.' Her father was 'six foot three, fair-haired, with movie star good looks and that beautiful aristocratic voice.' It was 'love at first listen'.

Herbert Murrill

While musical tastes at Bletchley ranged from middlebrow to high refinement, there were some among the codebreakers whose aesthetic taste and compositions were practically in the stratosphere. Herbert Murrill was an organ scholar who had devoted many years to the study and mastery of this instrument's complexity. He also wrote music, and some of his works are still performed in churches and cathedrals today, for example a choral setting of the *Magnificat* and an organ piece, *Carillon*. Murrill's career and life are further evidence of the attractiveness of musicians to the Bletchley establishment. There was clearly something about the way that a composer's mind worked that suited it to cryptographic work.

Murrill was also emblematic of the serious artistic generation that would emerge after the war. Born in London in 1909, he had studied at the Royal Academy of Music; before long, he was its Professor of Compositions. As well as his passion for organ music, he was a brilliant choral director. But he was cool as well: he also composed incidental music for plays by W. H. Auden. In 1936, he was recruited for a role that would disseminate his expertise across the nation: that of Music Programme Director for the BBC. It was through this particular grapevine that he was drawn into wartime intelligence, and in 1941 he arrived at Bletchley Park.

Naturally, as well as throwing himself into the challenge of decryption, Murrill set about forming a choral society for the Park. Nor did the shift work crowd out his creative musical inspiration: it was while at Bletchley that he composed what would become one of his most performed pieces: the *Nunc Dimittis in E*.

While most codebreakers were free to re-establish their lives shortly after the summer of 1945, Murrill was required to stay a year longer. But having belatedly emerged, he returned to the BBC and rose to become its Head of Music. Sadly, by 1951, he was ill with cancer, and had to leave his post, dying the following year aged 42.

Oliver Strachey

Amid a sea of youthful faces, Bletchley Park had its distinguished veterans too. One such, a 68-year-old man whose brother had been central to the Bloomsbury set, and who himself had lived a globetrotting life of culture and letters and music, shared an office in the mansion with the master codebreaker Brigadier John Tiltman (see page 194). Oliver Strachey was a superbly seasoned codebreaker himself, having begun this career in the First World War. While his brother Lytton was gracing the most shockingly progressive literary salons, Oliver was honing his expertise on everything from German to Japanese codes. There was adventure too: in 1916, he was sent to establish a cryptographic office in Egypt, and en route his ship was torpedoed and sunk.

There had been nothing in his younger years that especially pointed to this highly specialised career; except that he did demonstrate a flair for music. He had lived in Vienna for several years studying piano under Theodor Leschetizky, and yearned to be a concert pianist himself, but was never quite good enough. Strachey was also a child of the Empire; his father had been a colonial administrator.

There were faint echoes of this to be found in Strachey's cryptanalysis career. In 1941, he was sent over to Canada to take the lead in its codebreaking efforts. Before this, he had been leading ISOS – Intelligence Services – beginning to unpeel the Abwehr codes that concerned German agents being pulled into the Double Cross system. By 1942 he was back at the Park, analysing the communications about transport in Germany that revealed further details of the Final Solution.

The end of the war brought retirement (enforced – he had suffered a heart attack), and a gentle life in the genteel London suburb of Ealing, which ended in the spring of 1960, when he was 85.

Douglas Craig

Of all the soaring choral voices heard in and around the Park, that of Douglas Craig must have been especially distinctive. His talent for singing had been spotted at his school, Latymer Upper; he was performing in All Souls, Langham Place as a young teenager. But Craig's devotion to music went very much further; and decades after his codebreaking days, he went on to become involved with the running of Glyndebourne, the Welsh National Opera and most significantly, director of Sadlers Wells Theatre, not only rescuing it from decline and obsolescence, but repurposing it so that it became an established destination for many of the world's finest ballet companies.

Born in the dusty south London district of Vauxhall in 1916, when his jeweller father was fighting in the trenches, Craig (whose real name was actually Ernest Jones) soon proved himself an exceptionally bright pupil. And it was from Upper Latymer that he won a choral scholarship to St Catharine's College, Cambridge where he performed opera, joined the Footlights and studied languages. It was his linguistic dexterity that saw him receive the summons to Bletchley.

Like a great many other codebreakers, Craig was very serious about the Official Secrets Act, and he would not even tell close friends after the war exactly what it was that he had been doing. In later years, though, he did recount his profound delight at translating messages darting back and forth between Rommel in Africa and Hitler in Berlin. In this sense, codebreaking opened a curiously intimate and privileged window into history as it unfolded. But after the war, Craig was swift to resume — and develop — his life in music. Not only did he perform opera as a baritone, but he threw himself into the administrative side of the nation's resurging musical life. He spent some time as an assistant manager at Glyndebourne, gradually moving into directing from there. Craig went to the Welsh National Opera at a rich cultural moment in the 1960s. When he got to Sadlers Wells in 1970, vast changes were afoot; before Craig, the theatre had been a home for opera, but it was moving out to become the English National Opera at the Coliseum. In improving all the facilities so the venue could stage world-class ballet, Craig's far-sightedness — and extensive aesthetic interests — secured the future of an institution which remains popular and respected today.

In addition to all of this came the honours — the OBE, Fellow of the Royal College of Music, among others — without any of his colleagues (unless he ever ran into composer James Bernard) realising that honours were overdue in another corner of his life too.

GIFTED AMERICANS

Telford Taylor

The Nuremberg Trials – the post-war hearings at which judgement was handed down to those senior Nazis who had not committed suicide – changed the course of legal history. The very idea of them established new standards of universal rights (as well as defining the crime of genocide). Those who were prosecuting the hundreds of cases must have felt themselves to be standing in the glare of global spotlights, as they set about affirming the moral character of nations, and the morality of the years to come.

Chief among those prosecutors was a brilliant mind called Telford Taylor (by that stage, promoted to brigadier in the US Army). In the years that followed, his moral antennae remained fixed, even as America pursued new courses he considered extreme and wrong. As a Harvard lawyer, he courageously took a stand against the McCarthy Communist witch-hunts of the 1950s, and was later searingly critical of the Vietnam War and how it was fought. In his latter years, the opening of the archives threw new light on his own personal development, as the extent of his secret wartime work became known.

Amusingly, in the early 1940s, the initial reception given to Major Telford Taylor of the US Army by the codebreakers of Bletchley Park was wary. The UK and the US had agreed to work in tandem on intelligence, and by 1942 Taylor, then just in his early thirties, had arrived there to organise how best this might work. The British wariness was not personal: it was simply that in the wake of the First

World War, the Americans had seemed remarkably cavalier about publicising the success of their cryptological efforts. And there was gnawing anxiety that they might be tempted to do so again, and give the game away to the Nazis.

But Taylor was shrewd and sensitive, as well as alive to the complexities of codebreaking itself. It took him very little time to win the complete trust of his Bletchley colleagues. In turn, he had to adjust to the vagaries of British wartime life, and the truth behind the old British caricature of everything stopping for tea. He was especially pivotal in the preparations for D-Day, ensuring that Bletchley teams had a presence in senior American commands. Taylor worked with Hut 6, and the connection would follow him into his more visible and substantive post-war role. On his Nuremberg team he employed several linguists who had previously been working on the Bletchley Type-X code unravelling machines.

Throughout his subsequent legal and literary career in the post-war years, which saw him publish important books, including *The Breaking Wave*, about the war, and a memoir about the Nuremberg trials, he never forgot his Bletchley days; pleasingly, he formed an enduring friendship with Brigadier John Tiltman. And he was still happy to contribute to debates on the subject of what the codebreakers achieved, right up to his death in 1998, aged 90. His view, counter-intuitively, was that there was no one specific instance where Bletchley Park might have been said to have dramatically changed the course of the war; nonetheless, its work had made the fighting of that war a little 'better lubricated', and indeed ensured that the Battle of the Atlantic had a better outcome . . .

William Friedman

Although this most senior and experienced of American codebreakers only really passed through Bletchley Park on a series of flying visits, the colourful William Friedman is still a figure of some significance in the British codebreaking story. As well as his brokering the groundbreaking intelligence-sharing deal between the UK and the US — in its way vast and unprecedented — his recollections would provide the most intriguing snapshot of the Park's hierarchy, and how the establishment was run. Friedman, and his equally brilliant codebreaking wife Elizabeth, had themselves masterminded their way into various Japanese codes before the war; now he had the chance to see how the Enigma challenge was being met in the heart of unfamiliar English countryside.

Friedman was born in Russia in 1891; the following year, his family fled the anti-Semitic pogroms and he was brought up in Michigan. His taste for cryptography was triggered by the Edgar Allen Poe story 'The Gold Bug', which featured codes. By the First World War he was an expert sought out by the US military; in the interwar years, he was the architect of the US Signals Intelligence Service: the grand old man of codes. His 1943 visits to Bletchley were keenly anticipated.

The easier part of this was staying in London, where, as well as meetings with intelligence officials, he could make fussy trips to Liberty's department store in quests for a new pipe and a particular kind of walking stick. But the comforts of London were counterbalanced by the privations of his outings to Bletchley. He was put up in a pub, the Anchor, in Newport Pagnell. 'No facilities for laundry or bath', he wrote in some wonder. 'One young woman takes care of all.' The food, he noted, was excellent; but one detail irked him. 'Linen spotless but no napkins.' He was awoken the following morning by a maid bearing a pitcher of hot water, so that he might wash himself.

Yet balancing this was an acute reading of the politics between Bletchley's Commander Travis and the senior hierarchy. He was fascinated by the scale and the security of what had been achieved, and his admiration extended to the working conditions: he did not understand how they could endure 'the cold and the rain', the uncomfortable chairs and desks and the English habit of having windows wide open. 'They must be used to it,' he observed. One consolation: he was treated to epic lunches, invariably starting with 'Gin and French'. Alcohol was never in short supply.

Solomon Kullback

He was a mathematician who found himself on some unexpected paths throughout his life. A Brooklyn boy searching for escape, he ended up being introduced to the deepest levels of Bletchley Park. Solomon Kullback never lacked for enthusiasm, and one of his catchphrases would come to be adopted fondly by his British colleagues. At Bletchley as part of the team working to smash the Japanese codes, he was dazzled also by the immense successes won against the Nazi cryptographers.

Kullback had attended Boys High School in Brooklyn in an era very long before New York started to see any gentrification. He always had a talent for mathematics, and his original intention had been to be a schoolteacher; a friend, however, pointed him in a slightly more unusual direction. This came in the form of a civil service advertisement for 'Junior Mathematicians', which offered the then startlingly generous sum of $2,000 a year. He and his friend Abraham Sinkov sat the exam, and were subsequently inducted into William Friedman's crack team of secret cryptographers.

By the start of America's war, Kullback was now a major, and he and Sinkov had developed tremendous range and expertise. They were selected to set sail for England, and Bletchley, in 1942.

Kullback was noted especially for his fervid team spirit; he would frequently put in an unscheduled appearance on night shifts, to let Wrens and others know he was looking out for their welfare. His love of ten-pin bowling was slightly constrained at Bletchley: the town could offer only the genteel and aged option of Crown Green bowling, as opposed to the brash and bright alley variety. Balancing this was a tremendous British enthusiasm for all things American, best seen through the popularity of Hollywood films and the burning addiction to swing music.

Kullback celebrated each cryptographical breakthrough with the winning phrase 'We doo'd it!', borrowed from the film star Red Skelton. After the war, Dr Kullback at last became the teacher he had originally intended to be, though at the University of Washington rather than a tough Bowery school. The accident of falling into cryptography had changed the entire pattern of his life.

William Bundy

There used to be a time when some British people yearningly imagined that American society was somehow classless. While we had the paraphernalia of monarchy and lords and ladies, the US was seen as a sleek, smart meritocracy where anyone could rise to the top. In the nicest possible way, the life of Bostonian William Bundy was every bit as aristocratic and dynastic as that of the Duke of Gloucester. He did not lack for talent, though, and, as a man who served as an adviser in the early 1960s to Presidents Kennedy and Lyndon B. Johnson, and was later editor of the influential *Foreign Affairs* journal in the 1970s, he made a substantial mark on public life. That was not what he was proudest of, though.

Bundy was one of the US codebreakers happiest to make the transatlantic crossing; he took a certain delight in the eccentric Englishness of the establishment he joined. And while the work was never less than deadly serious, there was much in it to relish. The Bletchleyites relished him too: one described Bundy as 'everyone's ideal of the New England gentleman, tall, handsome, fresh-faced and courteous'. Certainly, Bundy's Bostonian roots and impeccable education at Groton and Harvard gave him polish. And polish was one of the attributes generally lacking at the Park.

What he also had, however, was an extraordinary family pedigree in espionage and intelligence. His father Harvey, working with US Secretary of War Henry Stimson, was deeply involved in the hyper-secret Manhattan Project, developing the atomic bomb at Los Alamos; and his mother Kay, who had taken to cryptology almost as a hobby, was recruited for the US equivalent of Bletchley – Arlington Hall in Virginia.

William Bundy was himself identified as a possible codebreaker while still at Harvard Law School; his studies were interrupted so that he could be enlisted into the US Army Signals Corps. Before he set sail for England, and Bletchley, he was briefed on the astounding coup against Enigma, so even before he arrived he had some respect for his more rackety-seeming English colleagues.

Earlier in the war, Bundy had married Mary Acheson, the daughter of Dean Acheson, who was later to become Secretary of State to President Kennedy. When Kennedy won the 1960 US Presidential election, his son-in-law was drawn into his inner circle. It was a small world. But that is not to belittle his many achievements, including later teaching at Princeton, or indeed the powerful intellect that underpinned his various career paths. All the way through, though, there was a pang of nostalgia.

'Although I have done many interesting things in my life and known many interesting people,' he declared in an interview, 'my work at Bletchley Park was the most satisfying of my career.'

MATHEMATICIANS AND PHILOSOPHERS

Alan Turing

Forget the name, for a moment. Here, in some senses, was the ultimate New Elizabethan: a man who in the 1950s was focused on bringing a new computer age into being while at the same time being able to run, in basic plimsolls, a marathon in two hours, forty minutes; a man who could engage Ludwig Wittgenstein in debate with brio and confidence, but also address BBC audiences with engaging and unlofty radio talks on the amazing prospects of artificial intelligence.

Here was a figure who, had he lived, would by the 1960s and 1970s surely have become a household name: an approachable, witty, good-humoured scientist who appeared to have an essential optimism about the possibilities of human nature. As it was, his fame would be posthumous and almost wholly connected with one institution. Yet even without that, he could have been famous many times over.

But what would Alan Turing's shade have made of his afterlife in the public eye? After decades where his name was known only in the most hermetic circles, he has risen to prominence as the very emblem of Bletchley Park: a brilliant mathematician and an abstracted innocent, with beguiling eccentricities, eventually driven to his death by a chilly Establishment. Turing's shade might now be bemused to see his handsome smiling face on postage stamps or bank notes; to see Benedict Cumberbatch's personation of him in *The Imitation Game*. He was just 26 when he was recruited to the Park at the outset of war;

barely turned 30 when he was sent to the US to share some of his outstanding expertise; and in 1954, at the University of Manchester, just 42 years old when he took his own life, following conviction for homosexuality (the term was 'gross indecency').

Yet might Turing's shade want to remind people that he was not just a mathematician, but a philosopher? The Turing Test was a hypothesis he devised involving the degree to which a computer might develop a reasoning intelligence indistinguishable in conversation from the human mind. This was not a mathematical leap, but a philosophical one, asking the deepest questions about what it is to be human, and indeed about whether the day could come when a human soul might inhabit a machine. How might his shade respond to the advent of voice-activated home computer devices that address their users in velvet female tones? In a sense, it was his thinking that made such developments possible.

Paradoxically, despite the technical brilliance he brought to Bletchley Park, Alan Turing was not its most successful codebreaker. What he did do, though, was envisage a world beyond the war that would eventually be changed by Artificial Intelligence. The melancholy nature of his death should not be allowed to overshadow the fact that – unlike the wartime scientists who worked on the Manhattan Project – Turing's vision was fundamentally bright. For him, computers had potential not to take over our lives, but to make them immeasurably better. In that sense, his legacy was overwhelmingly positive. His shade might also be pleased to note that his brilliance has been acknowledged by today's codebreakers at GCHQ.

Leslie Yoxall

Since codebreaking involved the hyper-focused mental ability to attack seemingly insoluble problems with lateral skill and cunning, might it also have given its practitioners an unfair advantage at croquet?

This certainly seemed to be the case with Leslie Yoxall. Born in Salford in 1914, and educated at Manchester Grammar School, Yoxall was another of the young recruits drawn in by the tractor beam of Gordon Welchman. Here was a further student at Sidney Sussex, Cambridge, although by the time his shoulder was tapped he had begun a career as a maths teacher at his old school. Britain's war demands were greater: and there were others at the Park who had need of his talents.

He was interviewed by Hugh Alexander and Alan Turing and joined Hut 8 in 1941, at the crucial moment in the Battle of the Atlantic when the codebreakers were struggling to crack U-boat messages and needed a serious breakthrough. The courageous capture of an Enigma machine and codebook from a torpedoed German submarine was invaluable, but Yoxall made his own contribution with a formula for analysing and unravelling codes that came to be termed Yoxallismus.

The former maths teacher developed such a taste for this life that he elected to continue it after the war, becoming a hugely valued addition to the team that was to reconstitute itself as GCHQ. His post-war work also took him to the US to spend ten years as a liaison between the UK and US intelligence communities. Although much of what is said about the 'special relationship' is sentimental nonsense, the alliance and friendship between British and American codebreakers was genuinely, historically, strong, with huge mutual respect.

And like all the finest codebreakers, Yoxall had a rich and unexpected hinterland, ranging from that lethal talent for croquet (an ability to see geometrical angles that others might not? Whatever the secret, Yoxall actually played in tournaments) to a passion for real ale, fine wine and birdwatching.

And rather movingly, he never forgot about his other love — teaching. He was always a member of the Association of Teachers of Mathematics, and when at last he retired after many successful years at GCHQ, he returned to his vocation, specialising in coaching and tuition. His life was even more of a shadowy secret than most other codebreakers', because for many years even the very existence of GCHQ was never uttered aloud. But he knew what he had helped to achieve. Sometimes discretion has its own satisfactions.

Jonathan Cohen

Some branches of philosophy resemble the most abstruse mathematics; more ordinary minds hesitate and stumble when faced with theories of probability, provability and propensity. Before the war, students and academics who were seen deep in thought on such matters were referred to as being in the 'absolute elsewhere'. But Jonathan Cohen, one of Bletchley Park's most distinguished philosophers, who spent his life wrestling with fearsomely complex propositions, was always very much in the present, a popular man whose penetrating intellect was allied to a friendly nature.

He came from a family of lively intellects. His father was Israel Cohen who, as well as being a journalist on the *Manchester Guardian*, was also General Secretary of the World Zionist Organisation. His son was born in 1923; by the late 1930s, he had won a place at Balliol College, Oxford to read Greats. He had barely started when he was plucked from there and thrown into the world of cryptology.

Cohen went a little further than most. After taking the crash course in Japanese, he was sent voyaging out to the Far East, and the Bletchley outstation at Colombo. The work was intense, but after the monochrome rainy frugality of England there was also a sensuous abundance about the place and its tastes and colours. Cohen was a lieutenant in Naval Intelligence, which gave him links across the oceans with Bond-author-to-be Ian Fleming.

And although it would be a stretch to say that the business of decryptions ignited his passion for logic and metaphysics, before the end of the war somewhere within Cohen's mind the fire was lit. Following his demobilised return to England, he went back to Balliol, but the new pathways of philosophy were what he sought. Academic posts followed in Edinburgh, and then in Dundee (a sharper contrast with the warmth and splendour of Colombo could not be imagined). His philosophy, centring on inductive reasoning and probability, was not purely abstract; there were theories that had applications for the law.

By the time he had returned to Oxford to take up a role as Fellow of Philosophy, he had written books such as *The Probable and the Provable* (published in 1977). He also became the general editor of the Clarendon Library of Logic and Philosophy. Cohen's was a life devoted to the very nature of meaning; the interlude of codebreaking Japanese ciphers amid tropical palms must have scrambled and re-scrambled a number of his youthful preconceptions about negotiating the labyrinth of language itself.

Keith Batey

For some recruits, there were doubts: was it really right that they got to spend their war well out of the range of any danger? Keith Batey was 20 years old, a student from Carlisle who had won a scholarship to Trinity College, Cambridge, when the Bletchley searchlight hit him in 1940. As a mathematician, he intuited at once the nature of 'the work' he was being drawn into. Like so many of his contemporaries, Batey had been on a shortlist of candidates updated by Gordon Welchman, and he was drafted into Hut 6 working on, among other things, the 'Brown' enigma codes which were filled with information about the German navigation beams used night after night by the Luftwaffe.

And this was the dilemma: Batey himself wanted to be an RAF pilot, actively defending the nation's skies against these fiery onslaughts. The difficulty was security – suppose he were to be shot down over enemy territory? And captured? And interrogated? There would be too strong a risk of the Bletchley secret getting out, and it was obviously imperative that the German military hierarchy not suspect their codes were being broken.

A compromise was reached. Batey was allowed to train with the Fleet Air Arm – if he were to crash, it would therefore be over water. Alas, his maiden flights inspired terror among those watching from terra firma, as his plane erratically swooped and dived, causing people to run for cover. The codebreaking day job it would have to be.

Mathematicians and Philosophers

It was just as well. Batey had terrific intellectual flair, applying it eventually to the codes that in 1944 would help the Park 'see' how the German military machine was responding on D-Day. It meant the Allies could make adjustments to their attack plans in real time.

And Bletchley Park brought one other vast bonus to Keith Batey, whose eye, from the moment he arrived, had been caught by 'all these nubile ladies'. He met Mavis Lever, a codebreaker from Dilly Knox's unit (see pages 144 and 184); they fell in love; their Park bosses, seeing blossoming romance, cunningly arranged for them to be seated together in the canteen. The romance was enduring.

After the war, Batey entered the Civil Service, with an early role in the Commonwealth Relations Office and later as secretary of the Royal Aircraft Establishment at Farnborough (even if his own piloting skills were erratic).

With retirement came the gradual prising open of the Bletchley story, and at some point in the late 1980s, Batey and his wife Mavis were – at last! – at liberty to tell each other what they had done in their respective Bletchley departments. Before that, they had both punctiliously observed the Official Secrets Act.

As interest in Bletchley's achievements blossomed, Batey and his wife found themselves in increasing demand for radio and book interviews and newspaper articles. His sly good humour, combined with his lustrous mathematical intellect, could leave less cerebral interviewers gaping like goldfish.

Oliver Lawn

In one sense, recruitment to Bletchley Park meant joining one of the most exclusive clubs in Britain. Even through the years of silence afterwards, it was still possible to take great, if unspoken, pride in having been a member. Oliver Lawn, drawn in as an undergraduate from Jesus College, Cambridge (again spotted by Gordon Welchman) went on to enjoy a rich career in the Civil Service (where in Whitehall he would occasionally pass, and exchange a few words with, his fellow codebreaker Keith Batey). But by the early 1990s there was also a late-life renaissance for him and his wife Sheila (also at the Park, see page 138). With the Enigma secret now disclosed – and the Park saved – an extraordinary form of celebrity descended.

The 85-year-old Lawn was, for instance, asked if he could solve the historical riddle of an inscription on the ancient Shugborough Monument in Staffordshire. Legend had it that the cryptic letters and images (including a tribute to the painter Nicholas Poussin), with some characters in mirror-writing, and all bewilderingly scrambled, pointed towards the location of the Holy Grail. Oliver and Sheila Lawn were photographed in the newspapers musing over this meaty puzzle. 'The inscription is obviously a classical reference,' said Mr Lawn. 'It's either Latin or Greek and based upon some historical happening. Why it's a mirror image is very strange.'

Mr and Mrs Lawn soon deduced that it was a heavily encoded love message, as opposed to a sinister mystery. But the real point was

Mathematicians and Philosophers

Mr Lawn's good humour. At Bletchley, he had sought respite from the rigours of Hut 6 and its round-the-clock shifts – he had been especially focused on the incredible volume of traffic from the Desert War that was enabling the codebreakers, and in turn Montgomery, to outmanoeuvre Rommel – by going to dances. Village hall hops were not enough, though, and he was very pleased when senior codebreaker Hugh Foss started the Highland Reels Society.

It transpired that young Mr Lawn had a genuine talent for Scottish dancing, which he honed across his years in the Park. It was also the reels that reeled in his wife-to-be. Sheila MacKenzie, hailing from Aberdeenshire, had joined Bletchley in 1943, and the Highland Reels Society seemed a perfect way to ward off homesickness. She saw the elegance and energy of Oliver Lawn's performances and was smitten; he likewise with her.

As the years wore on, continuing disclosures about Bletchley enabled Oliver Lawn to comprehend the full scale of his side of the codebreaking operation, and its impact on the war in North Africa, and in 2012 he and his wife finally managed to discuss it with the Queen when she made a special visit to Bletchley Park, outside a peeling, crumbling Hut 6. Happily, and thanks not least to Oliver Lawn's efforts to help the Park's resurrection, that hut is now fully restored.

John Herivel

We expect the course of history to be changed on the battlefield or in the Cabinet room, but not, generally speaking, in the front parlour of a modest dwelling near a busy provincial railway junction. Yet on one freezing cold night, a young man resting in front of the glowing, ticking fire after his shift fell into a meditative trance. Looking at the coals, he let his imagination roam across to Germany, and then other theatres of war. He was imagining the operators of the Enigma machines, and how they actually went about setting up their machines. At a certain point, the young man had a lightning flash of insight both psychological and mathematical. It was so intense that he could hardly wait to see if his theory would work.

The young man was John Herivel, born in Belfast and another Welchman protégé, and the epiphany came to inform a procedure known at Bletchley as the Herivel Tip. It was based on the idea that those who operated the Enigma machines – with their daily instructions for re-setting the wheels and the settings – might actually be rather lazy about choosing the so-called three-letter indicators that would form the first test message of the day; that in practice the operator would only move the rotors by a few letters, and that these indicators would form clusters. If Bletchley could get hold of a great mass of first daily messages – the informal greetings sent by operators – they could get a crowbar into all those days' codes.

This was in 1940, before mechanisation came to Bletchley, and it is no exaggeration to say that the Herivel Tip made it possible to

Mathematicians and Philosophers

read vast quantities of so called 'Red' ciphers from the German army as the invasion of France and preparations for the Battle of Britain got under way. At last Bletchley Park was in business, and the psychological boost to the codebreakers was vast. Thanks to Herivel, they could see that even working by hand, nothing was insoluble.

His post-Bletchley life was marked with one searing moment of sadness. When his father was dying, Herivel was still bound by the Official Secrets Act, forbidden to even mention Bletchley Park. Herivel, born in Belfast in 1918, was another Welchman protégé. From his father's point of view, his son had opted to remain a civilian throughout the war with no explanation; now, with his father on his deathbed, Herivel had to endure the accusation that he had done and achieved nothing with his life. Even at that moment of mortality, the son refused to break the vow of secrecy.

It can only be hoped that, as he reached the end of his own life, after a fine career of university teaching and writing, John Herivel at last had the satisfaction and the pride of the wider world knowing that he had in fact made a substantial difference. The tribute had been paid by Gordon Welchman himself: without Herivel and his 'tip', he insisted, the consequences would have been 'disastrous'.

Peter Hilton

One of the more moving aspects of the Bletchley Park story is the way the members of this intensely secret community maintained friendships and close contacts in the years following their wartime feats. The codebreakers may never have been allowed the luxury of reunions – at least, not until the turn of the century, when Bletchley Park inaugurated an annual Veterans' Day – but they had bonds forged in the most extraordinary adversity.

Peter Hilton, just 17 when the war broke out, was initially convinced that his destiny lay elsewhere. In 1940 he won a scholarship to Queen's College, Oxford to study mathematics. But as soon as he could, Hilton enlisted for the army. The recruiters at Bletchley Park were having none of it. Apart from anything else, the young man had taught himself German in addition to his official studies – the combination of linguistic and mathematical flair could not be squandered. Naturally Hilton was very modest about it all, later recalling that 'I was the only person who turned up for the interview' for this unspecified job and for that reason 'they jumped up and said, "Yes, you must come."'

By 1942, Hilton was in Hut 8, at the point when finally they were starting to make headway in the battle of the naval ciphers. Then came a move to work with the Heath Robinson machine. As well as a penetrative mind, Hilton had the most unusual talent for visualising streams of information: he could hold in his mind the output from simultaneously running teleprinters and form cohesive meaning from apparent chaos. 'For me,' he recalled years later, 'the real excitement was this business of getting two texts out of one sequence of gibberish. I never met anything quite so exciting, especially since you knew these were vital messages.'

Perhaps this might also explain his freakish ability to devise epically long palindromes. One effort that he produced in his Bletchley leisure hours ran: 'Doc, note: I dissent. A fast never prevents a fatness. I diet on cod.' The Lorenz encrypters in Germany clearly never stood a chance. Hilton also enjoyed his chess battles with Alan Turing. Unlike Peter Twinn, he had no idea of his colleague's sexual orientation, but in the 1950s he was furious that the authorities set out to prosecute his wartime colleague for gross indecency; quite apart from the inhumanity, this was no way to treat 'an authentic genius'.

It was at Bletchley Park that Hilton got to know Professor Max Newman, and after the war, when he returned to Oxford to continue his studies, he knew his next move would be to follow the Professor to the University of Manchester. The Professor was ambitious: Manchester was to rival Oxbridge.

Hilton's own speciality was algebraic topology, or specifically the mathematics of shapes. Married to the actress Margaret Mostyn, he was only in his early thirties when he became a senior lecturer. The tendrils of that community stretched far: in 1962 Hilton was recruited to work in the US, first at Cornell University, and subsequently at other prestigious academic departments.

He remained in America for the rest of his life. Did the scale and dazzle of that country compensate at all for what he was missing so badly? For the fact was that after the mad intensity of those Bletchley years, it took Professor Hilton a long time to adjust to the grey British post-war landscape – if indeed he ever did.

Shaun Wylie

Many at Bletchley Park made friends for life, but there were also paths that had fatefully crossed before the war, friendships struck that would add to the richness of Bletchley's intellectual lustre. When Shaun Wylie, a 27-year-old schoolmaster, received the summons to the Buckinghamshire estate, it was in part a wonderful reunion with Alan Turing, whom he had first met in America a couple of years previously. Wylie was there studying at Princeton (having previously won a scholarship to New College Oxford), working in the mathematical field of topology.

Arriving at Bletchley in 1940, he was hurled into the complexities of cribs and Bombe machines, and then later into the labyrinth of Tunny. He was a terrific addition to Hut 8, both because of his cleverness and because of his lightness of touch. One of his talents was the ability to laugh off even the most demonic pressure. Whereas some codebreakers were prone to introversion, Wylie was a brilliant communicator.

And Bletchley introduced him to the love of his life. Odette Murray was a Wren working on the complex Colossus machines. Decades later, when the curtains of secrecy had parted, they both contributed essays to the burgeoning literature on what had been achieved at the Park.

And Wylie, like a few of his colleagues, found that once inducted into this hermetic world, one could never entirely leave it behind. Although his post-war academic career glittered with distinction – as well as being a much-loved lecturer who could make the fiercest mathematical propositions a source of amusement, he had helped Watson and Crick with some of the modelling of the form of the double helix – Wylie also had a parallel secret career, as Chief Mathematician for Bletchley's successor organisation, GCHQ. It was Wylie who foresaw a new age where vast quantities of electronic communications would be criss-crossing the world every second. He saw how there could be difficulties encrypting such messages; but he also saw the potential for unlocking new secrets.

There was a physicality to Wylie too; like Bletchley's original director Alastair Denniston, he was a gifted hockey player. In 1938, he played in international tournaments for Scotland. He also had the skittish wit common to those who enjoy devising cryptic crosswords; his own creations ran in the *Listener* magazine.

In addition to all of this, in the early 1980s he was one of the founder members of the Social Democratic Party – all in all, a wonderfully wide portfolio for a GCHQ operative. Although he was fundamentally modest, he was at the core of Bletchley's success. As Hugh Alexander said of him: 'Except for Turing, no-one made a bigger contribution to the success of Hut 8 than Wylie; he was easily the best all-rounder in the section, astonishingly quick and resourceful and contributed a great deal to theory and practice in a number of different directions.'

MEN AND WOMEN OF LETTERS

Angus Wilson

Literary stars dazzle, then fade, then, as the years turn, sometimes acquire rediscovered lustre. One of Bletchley Park's most intense and colourful recruits is due that return to fashion. Sir Angus Wilson wrote novels and short stories that, for a time in the 1950s and 1960s, dominated middle-class bookshelves: piercing and sometimes bitter parables of the shifting post-war social and sexual landscape. Naturally none of his readers would have guessed what he had done during the war. But he brought that intellectual acuteness — and his mercurial temperament — to the work. Of the thousands who worked at the Park, Wilson was, in manner and in dress, among the most distinctive. In the town of Bletchley there were those who would remember him decades afterwards.

Born in Sussex in 1913, the youngest of six siblings, Wilson soon acquired a certain local renown as a young man by way of his dyed hair and scarlet nail polish. He never hid his homosexuality, even though it was then illegal. After studying at Oxford, he had a spell at the Foreign Office, but gave it up and found himself a berth in the British Library. By the outbreak of war Wilson, with his imaginative facility with language, was on the Bletchley radar. But he found his time there very difficult; he could not find any way of separating himself from the searing intensity of the work, and felt under continuous pressure. This brought on a breakdown. Whether throwing a bottle of ink at a Wren or throwing himself into the lake at the front of the house, his symptoms caused bewilderment among fellow codebreakers. Eventually the directorate recognised his suffering, and he was guided towards therapy.

Even amid all the other colourful Bletchley figures, Wilson became talked of in the town because of his flamboyant dress sense: indigo shirts matched with tangerine bow ties. After the war, he returned to work at the British Library – at that time still in its magnificent Reading Room at the heart of the British Museum – but his literary career was on the launch pad. There was the short story collection *The Wrong Set*, mould-breaking in its frank depiction of homosexuality, and novels such as *Anglo-Saxon Attitudes*.

Very quickly he was at the centre of the literary establishment. He bestrode the Royal Society of Literature, and was one of the founding forces behind the University of East Anglia and its then creative writing course, nurturing young talent like Ian McEwan and Rose Tremain. His long-term partner Tony Jarrett was, he insisted, always to be recognised as such, even before legalisation of homosexuality in 1967.

Yet in the 1980s Angus Wilson's work fell out of literary fashion, and by the turn of the century his work was largely out of print. A revival is overdue, not least because the millions who are now fascinated by Bletchley's history would enjoy reading the works of one of its most diverting figures, packed as they are with close-up social historical detail.

Christine Brooke-Rose

The fame may have come to Angus Wilson, but he was not the most interesting novelist at Bletchley Park. That must surely be Christine Brooke-Rose who, while never becoming a household name, nevertheless won prizes for her exactingly deconstructionist fiction. It is more than possible that the experience of working with codes – itself the pursuit of meaning in deconstructed language – inspired her thinking about the novel and propelled her towards her eventual professorship at the University of Paris, where she was among some of the more radical literary thinkers turning the form inside out and back again.

Born in Geneva in 1923 – her father was English, her mother Swiss American – Christine Brooke-Rose was taken to live in London in the 1930s. When war came, she joined the WAAF, and it was her ease with linguistics that pulled her towards Bletchley Park. Her main role was translating decrypted German messages, but the formless anarchy of the encryptions seized her imagination. She had joined Bletchley having only passed her school exams. After the war, she went up to Somerville College, Oxford to read English.

Her first novels came in the 1950s; *The Languages of Love* and *The Sycamore Tree* conjured a world of polo-neck sweaters and sooty London cafés. But it was in 1966 that she won the highbrow James Tait Black Memorial Prize for her novel *Such*, presenting the metaphysical (and astrophysical) experiences of an astronomer following his death.

The move to Paris academia in the 1970s, when all the talk was of post-structuralism and the Death of the Author, brought forth from her more novels at a level of abstruseness that would have made James Joyce clap his forehead with vexation. The niche sales were neither here nor there; the exploration of form, and all its philosophical implications, was the point.

She described her time at the Park as 'a first training of the mind, a first university', and said that it also opened her up to the viewpoint of the other. Additionally, in another pleasing echo of Bletchley, and of the dawn of the computer age, she wrote intensely literary science fiction, some involving sentient silicon. In all of this was a giddying exultation in intellect: the lifeblood of Bletchley.

Vernon Watkins

In some sense, the Enigma codes were language turned inside out, words disguised as anarchic gibberish. The task of tearing away that disguise and restoring the rightful letters had been taken on largely by mathematicians, but the task could be appreciated by poets too. Bletchley Park succeeded in recruiting one of the finest poets of his generation.

A good friend of Dylan Thomas, Vernon Watkins had already found published success when he arrived in the early 1940s. Steeped in symbolism, and concerned with what he described as 'the conquest of time', the 'romantic paganism' of his work was admired by T. S. Eliot. For many years after the war, Watkins' time at Bletchley was not referred to; instead, he was simply described as having worked for the RAF. But it was a formative time in another crucial respect: it was at the Park that he met his wife to be, Gwen Davies, who was serving there as a Wren.

Watkins was also one of the few people to have been recruited to the Park from behind a bank counter. He had started working at his local branch of Lloyd's in Swansea in 1928. But it was not so much this as his linguistic flair – fluent in German, Watkins had read French at Cambridge – that made him a suitable cryptography candidate.

After the war, though, he could not wait to return to his home on the Gower Peninsula, where he and his new wife brought up a large family. Even as his poetic successes multiplied – volumes included

The Lamp and the Veil and *The Lady With The Unicorn* — he was more than happy to remain as a bank teller; the routine of the work gave him regular income and also the space to dream. With his published poetry winning prizes, he retained his daily routine, including a quiet lunch spent reading in a local café, and became what he described as 'the oldest cashier' in banking. Yet when he retired in 1966, he was invited to the US to become Visiting Professor of Poetry at the University of Washington. It was there that he died relatively young, aged 61, his codebreaking life unknown to all except his codebreaking wife.

Henry Reed

The atmosphere at Bletchley was conducive to satirists; here in the midst of the life-and-death work was a rich panorama of social comedy. And the poet Henry Reed, who came to the Park via Naval Intelligence, had the keenest eye for the occasional absurdities of war. His most famous poem, 'Naming of Parts', was inspired by his initial drafting into the army, and military equipment training in the Royal Ordnance Army Corps.

Born in Birmingham in 1914, and completing his education at the city's university, where he specialised in the works of Thomas Hardy, Reed had been encouraged in the 1930s by the poet Louis MacNeice to explore a literary career. What brought Reed sharply to the attention of Bletchley in 1941 was his preternatural flair for picking up languages. He was one of the recruits directed to work upon the seemingly intractable Japanese codes. Such was the saturation in the language that the literary critic Walter Allen would later write that Reed intended 'to devote every day for the rest of his life to forgetting another word of Japanese'.

It was also at Bletchley that he was to make the friends and contacts that would help him build a prolific post-war career at the BBC (sometimes throughout the war he was sent to London on highly classified liaison). Reed's sharp intellect was worn lightly; after Bletchley Park, he began to specialise in radio plays, and took on some of the parts himself. As he took on full-time work with the BBC, and later diversified into critical work and literary translations, his poetry remained in the shadows. He died in 1986, aged 71. Several years later, his collected poems were published posthumously.

S. Gorley Putt

While much of the codebreaking was about mathematics, the actual business of what the unravelled messages said was about the ambiguities and hidden codes of language itself. Gorley Putt (who was most insistent that no-one used his actual first name, which was Samuel) was an expert in the novels of Henry James and friends with the pioneering and pre-eminent literary critic F. R. Leavis. More than this: as a Naval Intelligence officer at Bletchley, he brought direct experience of life on the waves in a battleship. As well as being alive to linguistics, he also understood very well the language of the sea.

His enthusiasm for the navy was striking, given that his own father had lost his life in 1918 after his boat had been torpedoed by the enemy. Gorley Putt, born in 1913, was brought up by his mother in the Devon seaside town of Brixham. There was, said Putt lightly of the post-First World War years, 'a craze for single-parent families'. Following his grammar school education in Torquay, Putt won a scholarship to Christ's College, Cambridge to study a relatively new academic discipline: English Literature. It was Leavis who had given the subject some serious academic heft. Putt flourished and subsequently got the chance to study at Yale, which imprinted him with a great love and admiration for the US.

When war came, Putt volunteered for the navy, and it was as an ordinary seaman that in 1940 he embarked upon a destroyer protecting a convoy. By the following year, he was in Intelligence at the

Park. But he still found the time to write his first book *Men Dressed as Seamen*, which was published in 1943.

The post-Bletchley years brought great involvement with the Commonwealth Fund, setting up and fostering international fellowships, and he returned to Christ's College, becoming senior tutor. His expertise on the novels of Henry James was rich and sought-after. He was an evangelist for the finer things, wine included, noted for his smart (though slightly stained) white dinner jacket, whipped out at the slightest chance. He remained devoted to his students even at a time – the 1970s – when many of them were making Maoist nuisances of themselves. His time at Bletchley Park had taught him what can happen to young people forced together in a hothouse atmosphere. 'One after another,' he wrote later, 'in one way or another, we would all go off our rockers.'

Beryl Lawry

Translation is a delicate and under-sung art. It is not simply a matter of transposing one word with another; it is about capturing nuance and intention, emphasis and sensibility. It is a form of codebreaking in itself: taking sentences, breaking them down, then rebuilding and reassembling them so that their meaning is conveyed with crystalline purity.

For Beryl Lawry, the business of translation carried extra weight and responsibility: first, through working with decoded German messages at Bletchley Park and then, after the war, bringing her linguistic skills to the Nuremberg Trials. In the former, complete accuracy was vital, since the intelligence was being used out in the field in situations of life and death; in the latter because the principle of justice had to be seen to be inviolate when passing judgement on Nazi murderers.

To the woman born Beryl Beswick in Stockport in 1923, all this was a fragment of a full and rich life. Her youthful ease with languages won her a place at the University of London, and it was there that, after the war, she gained a Double First in German and French. But her pre-war studies were interrupted by the letter telling her to report to Station X. How could such a talent not be drawn into the vortex of Bletchley?

The work in the Naval section was exacting, but her diligence was noted and appreciated, for it led to a request for her to travel to Germany after the war to work at the Nuremberg Trials. This appealed to her very strongly on a moral basis: the chance to participate in a process that would demonstrate to the world that the Allies believed above all in fair trials, and thus set the moral tone internationally for the years to come.

After this, her internationalist interests were developed by a new career with the British Council, a body established to strengthen links with different nations across the world. There was some drama when her posting to Prague in communist Czechoslovakia was rudely terminated and she and her fellow Council colleagues were expelled from the country after a tit-for-tat Cold War intelligence row. It was with one of her colleagues – Tod Lawry – that she fell in love.

Their subsequent careers took them from west to east; in Hong Kong, she became adept with Cantonese. This adaptability – and adventurousness – was a long way from the domestic lives that most post-war British women were obliged to live. Bletchley Park widened the frontiers of possibility for great numbers of its female recruits.

Carmen Blacker

How can the hatred ignited by war be extinguished? How can enemies perceived as being demonically cruel be seen once more as human? It is unlikely Carmen Blacker would ever have regarded her own calling in such terms: she was an ardent scholar of Japanese language, literature, culture and history. The war brought with it atrocities committed by the Japanese army that continued to reverberate through British popular culture and politics for many years, yet it was Carmen Blacker, immediately after the war, who sought to promote fresh and deeper understanding of a society that was obscure to many.

Her interest in Japan had been sparked when she was a child (she was born in Surrey in 1924), and continued throughout her schooldays at Benenden. It was from there that she was plucked, aged 18, from the sixth form to join the Japanese codebreaking operation at Bletchley. The exhausting requirements of her job were never enough to quell her appetite for extra study; in precious hours of leave, she turned to translating a notoriously difficult eighteenth-century Japanese work of literature called *The Straw Sandal*.

What marked Carmen Blacker out at Bletchley, and in her distinguished academic career afterwards, was steadfast self-belief and a lack of fear when it came to standing up to authority figures. The first of those at Bletchley was a Miss Moore, who conducted the interviews. Given that she had been summoned in complete secrecy, with no idea what the job was – except that there were night shifts – Carmen asked boldly why night shifts were necessary.

'You do *want* this job, don't you?' replied Miss Moore tightly.

Blacker recalled she was tempted to answer back: all that stopped her was the general convention in those days that one avoided doing so openly. But conditions at Bletchley nettled her: the pay was low (on account, she was told, of her age); there was no heating in her billet bedroom; she was only allowed one hot bath a week. Conversely the work could be exultantly exciting: she remembered her first, dazzled sight of an Enigma machine, marvelling at its ingenuity.

But by the end of the war, she regretted not being on the German codes; for by contrast, she could not see how her work in the Japanese section was of the same practical help. Frustrated, she was advised to fill her spare time by learning Chinese.

After the war, she first studied Politics, Philosophy and Economics, but within a few years was at the University of Tokyo, immersing herself in her true love of Japanese letters and art. She returned to teach Japanese at Cambridge and her books – among them *The Catalpa Bow: A Study In Shamanistic Practices in Japan*, for which she underwent pilgrimages and attended festivals – were much admired. And as well as her OBE and a slew of fellowships, she was given the Order of the Precious Crown by the Japanese government in recognition of her efforts to bring greater understanding and warmth to Anglo-Japanese dealings. She also worked on books with her husband Michael Loewe, whom she had met at Bletchley, and who had his own distinct hinterland.

Professor Alison Fairlie

Could there be circumstances under which codebreaking could be seen as a branch of literary criticism? There is the laser-beam focus on the 'text' (scrambled as it is); the probe for 'meaning'; the exploration of ambiguities thrown up within the decrypted messages (the language might have been rendered plain, but thereafter, certain words or phrases would continue to cause bafflement); and the fitting of the 'text' (or message) into the wider context around it, in an attempt to understand the intentions and motivations of the 'text''s author. All in all, much like studying James Joyce's *Finnegans Wake*.

Alison Fairlie brought a weight of literary and critical expertise to her role at Bletchley Park. Indeed, it was her study of French poetry that actively helped her in the trying business of cross-referencing enemy military terms. She was lucky to have survived the early months of the war to make it to Bletchley at all, and it was her passion for French poetry that almost got her killed.

Born in Shetland in 1917, and brought up thereafter in Ardrossan, an Ayrshire coastal town, when her vicar father's ministry changed, Alison always had a restless appetite for learning. By the late 1930s, she was ensconced at St Hugh's, Oxford, having sat her degree in Medieval and Modern Languages. It was at this time that she decided to join the Communist Party and read the *Daily Worker*. This, according to friends, was less to do with a belief in Marxism than simply a means of opposing the fascism of Hitler, Mussolini and Franco.

Her studies in French poetry (with special reference to Lecomte de Lisle) took her to Paris in the early weeks of 1940. As the Nazi war machine was fast approaching, she was apparently initially reluctant to leave, because she could not believe that the invaders would interfere with the Bibliothèque Nationale. But when the time for escape came – she and her friends decided on a route through Bordeaux – there was real danger. They had a nightmare time trying to find a boat that would take them across the Channel, and when they did (an old cargo tub filled with filthy coal and grain), they faced bombing on top of gruesome seasickness. Throughout it all, she recalled, she and her young friends laughed: a survival reflex. Aside from the falling bombs, the crossing itself, on 'glittering seas', was very pleasant.

Recruited at last for Bletchley, she was assigned for a department known as 'the Watch', which dealt with mysteries in decrypted messages: terms that could not be fathomed. This involved a library of technical manuals in various languages (so many of the terms were parts for various weapons), and it turned out that some obscure words used by the poet Lecomte de Lisle came up in these decrypts.

The post-war years brought bracing academia: lecturing in French at Girton College, Cambridge; becoming a much admired (if occasionally frightening) tutor; professorship in 1972; Fellowship of the Royal Academy and a slew of other accolades. The avid learning, and laser focus on the minutiae of literary texts, never diminished. The interval at Bletchley was not so much a career break as continuity.

POLYMATHS AND ENTREPRENEURS

Dennis Babbage

Perhaps it is unsurprising that a man who had mastered the most complex new theorems of geometry should be a whizz on the snooker table. But Dennis Babbage was not just brilliant at potting blacks; he could also hit shots with the cue held behind his back. At Bletchley Park, this uncalled-for talent drew gasps of admiration from young colleagues. But it was his ability to see the cat's cradle of all the different cryptological challenges and systems that led to him being drawn into one of the Park's most senior roles as war broke out in 1939.

Babbage, born in 1909 and educated at St Paul's, had won a scholarship to Cambridge in 1927 and been showered with prizes almost from the moment he arrived. In 1936 he became a lecturer at the university. He was a man who could be tongue-tied, and even on occasion rather shy, but discussions could suddenly explode into life as he quoted extensively from classical literature.

What Bletchley needed was not just the ability to break codes; it also needed an organisational framework that could anticipate encryption developments yet to come. And so Babbage was appointed the head of the Park's Research Unit, and gained the title of Chief Cryptographer aged just 30. After the war, he was awarded the OBE for his secret services.

And he was swift to return to Magdalene College, Cambridge, where in time he eventually became Senior Proctor. His uncanny ability on the snooker table was matched by an unnerving eye on

Polymaths and Entrepreneurs

tennis and squash courts; this had been wryly noted by fellow codebreaker Gordon Welchman, a furiously competitive man.

The competition extended beyond the court: in the early 1980s, when Welchman had published his own account of the Bletchley story, which ,for reasons of official secrecy, was received so badly by the British government, Babbage wrote him a lengthy – though gentle – letter detailing a technical mistake about one of the pioneering codebreaking techniques; the error was elucidated partly through algebraic means. Secret the work may have been, and entirely based around teamwork, but the codebreakers were still sensitive about where ideas had originated and where credit should go, and on this occasion Babbage was arguing essentially that in one particular case, Dilly Knox (see page 186) was most in need of praise. In other words, Bletchley history came to read like amusing collegiate bickering. Alas, Babbage could only claim slender bloodline links to the illustrious nineteenth-century computer pioneer Charles Babbage, but the symmetry was always pleasing nonetheless.

Peter Calvocoressi

There were among the codebreakers those whose intellectual passions and interests were so wide-ranging it was possible to wonder how they found the time. One such figure was a historian/lawyer/publisher/musician/academic/politician/campaigner against censorship and apartheid whose name was Peter Calvocoressi. He had been told at university that his exotic-sounding surname would prove a hindrance in public life. Calvocoressi went on to prove otherwise. And his time at Bletchley demonstrated his energetic ability to have life ordered in the way he preferred.

Born in Karachi (in what was then British India) in 1912, Calvocoressi was of Greek heritage; his parents came to Britain and the young student won a scholarship to Eton, proceeding from there to Balliol College, Oxford, where his passion for history earned him a First. He was unofficially disbarred from a career in the Foreign Office by his Greek background; happily, this sort of obstacle did not prevent him being picked out to join the codebreakers of Hut 3 in 1941. (Though even this was fortuitous: he had volunteered for the army and had seen, on a desk, a note summing him up as 'No good, not even for intelligence'; the assumption was that he was unfit owing to an old head injury from a car accident. But it was then suggested to him that he should write directly to the Air Ministry, and that his fluency in German and French might be of use. It most certainly was).

Calvocoressi specialised in Luftwaffe intelligence, decrypting and analysing the communications and manoeuvres of Goering and his lieutenants. He rose to become head of the Air section. He was present for one of Bletchley's great coups: the intelligence that pinpointed the feared German battleship *Bismarck*. In part, the ship's position was betrayed by Luftwaffe messages discussing whether to give it air cover. It was sunk by the British shortly afterwards. 'Ultra took the blindfold off our eyes,' wrote Calvocoressi, 'so that we could see the enemy in detail in a way in which he could not see us.'

After the war, Calvocoressi became deeply immersed in the Nuremberg trials (in part, helping to prepare Telford Taylor for his own prosecuting role). He also ran the Chatham House institute, joined the board of publishers Chatto and Windus, became Editor-in-Chief of Penguin Books, was a reader in International Relations at the University of Sussex, a founder member of Amnesty International, and a man devoted to music.

While at Bletchley, he swiftly grew tired of peeling-wallpaper lodgings, and so he bought nearby Guise House (a temporary measure that lasted decades) where he moved with his wife, children and a range of musical instruments, so that codebreaker lodgers could play string quartets.

Frank Birch

Sometimes the combination of intellect and energy causes an overflow of activity and achievement. The life of Francis (Frank) Birch would have been remarkable enough even without his key contributions to the success of British codebreaking across two generations. He was a historian and a mesmerising lecturer. But he was also a comic talent, who had acting in his blood. So, unlike his peers in the Bletchley Park directorate, Birch could boast of having starred at the London Palladium and then, after the war, of having appeared in a film farce with Sid James. Curiously, given this unstoppable ebullience, he was also regarded at Bletchley as something of a martinet.

Birch, born in 1889, attended Eton and Kings College, Cambridge. It was there that he took a Double First in History, and where the academic side of his life began; he became a Fellow and then a lecturer at quite a young age. His lectures were fiercely compelling: full of gestures and effects, this was history as performance art. The Great War drew him into the Navy, and from there to Room 40 intelligence. The inter-war years brought a return to Cambridge, but also the development of his mania for theatre: first expressed in university productions, but then transferred to the London stage, where he performed in the original version of the farce *One Man, Two Guvnors* (latterly revived in the West End with James Corden), and in pantomime essayed a sensational Widow Twankey.

Nazism casting a lengthening shadow over Europe brought Birch back into codebreaking where, overseeing the Naval section, he surveyed the new generation of recruits with a blend of admiration and crossness. The young mathematicians Alan Turing and Peter Twinn were, whatever their talents, in his view 'untidy' and clumsy, and prone to skittishness. The intense stress of the Battle of the Atlantic brought Birch's salty temper further to the fore. Yet he also commanded respect.

After the war, living in London amid the elegant streets of Knightsbridge, he maintained strong links with what was to become GCHQ: as a historian, he wrote the (initially classified) wartime history; as Deputy Director, he surveyed the new Cold War landscape. But this also remarkably left him spare time to appear in BBC television plays and a film with George Cole. Few among the codebreakers could boast of such a distance between their public and their secret lives. He died in 1956.

John Cairncross

The vetting procedures at Bletchley were beyond tight: Frank Birch had been instrumental in ensuring that Kim Philby, later unmasked as one of the Cambridge Spies, was never recruited. But another of those spies did slip through the gates. And whenever he was due leave, he would catch the train to London to meet his Soviet handler in the west London borough of Ealing.

John Cairncross, a shining Scottish intellect and young rising star at the Foreign Office, had been selected for Bletchley in 1943. No-one suspected that in the 1930s, as a Cambridge post-graduate, he had been approached by the communist James Klugman to provide intelligence to Stalin's Russia.

Yet there are traitors who would argue to their final breath that theirs was not treachery at all. Cairncross later claimed that his motivation had been shock that a wartime ally, as Russia then was, had been deliberately kept in the dark about Bletchley and the crystalline intelligence it had decrypted. Even if anyone were to accept that, however, the passing of information about Bletchley itself was lethally dangerous: there was no guarantee that that secret would not seep out via the Soviets to the Nazis. It was only some years after the war that the authorities pinpointed Cairncross as 'the Fifth Man'. He had gone to work for the Treasury, and was dismissed in 1952.

Yet this towering – and glowering – intellect found fresh avenues to explore. He worked for the United Nations Food and Agriculture Organisation, taught at Northwestern University, became a great authority on – and translator of – French literary classics published by Penguin (his translations of Racine's dramas are still in print), and also gave economic advice to Italian banks.

Cairncross, who was born in a village near Glasgow in 1913, always seemed to plough a lonely furrow. Ironically, when he was at Trinity College, Cambridge in the 1930s, it was another Cambridge Spy, Anthony Blunt, who had considered him a possibility as another recruit but regretted that in social terms, the lower-middle-class Cairncross was 'not a gentleman'. In other words, Cairncross perhaps had more reason than his fellow traitors for loathing the oppressive snobbery which even they perpetuated.

Eric Jones

The Park drew figures from many walks of life, yet startlingly few from the world of commerce. One of its most effective and popular recruits, who went on to build on Bletchley's success after the war, hailed from a background of textile manufacturing. Sir Eric Jones (the knighthood came later, and discreetly, for codebreaking triumphs) found that his flair for organisation and nimble systems was as well suited to the shadowy realm of cryptography as it was to his natural habitat of boardrooms. In both domains, he naturally rose to the top, and remained remarkably popular while doing so.

He was born in 1907, and went to King's School in Macclesfield. There was no university for Jones; he was impatient to immerse himself in his family's textile business. But these horizons were not quite broad enough, and in the mid-1920s he set up his own business as a textile merchant, which grew rapidly, right across the north and the Midlands too, bringing a wide variety of new contacts.

The war with Hitler meant that Jones handed over the business to a manager while he himself headed into the RAF. He was swiftly siphoned into the Air Ministry, which was in need of technocratic skill, and there he was spotted for Bletchley. Soon Jones was heading up Hut 3, setting up means by which the intensely secret intelligence produced by the Park could be most effectively disseminated to those who needed it without compromising its provenance.

A large man, prone to loudly tailored suits, Jones had a pleasing, sincere manner that made him a perfect candidate for helping to construct the special encryption relationship with his American counterparts, who adored him. He was to be honoured with the US Legion of Merit.

The end of the war might have brought a twitch on the thread from his old business, yet Jones decided to stay on. And when Sir Edward Travis retired in 1952, Eric Jones became the Director of GCHQ. He found Cheltenham intensely agreeable, buying a manor house nearby. After eight years of Cold War manouevres, he too decided to step down, but this was by no means the end of his working life. He threw himself once more into commerce, and into smoky boardrooms, with a variety of directorships.

One key to his success was his apparently boundless enthusiasm for life generally. Whether unravelling the knots of encryption or re-landscaping his garden, navigating complex diplomacy with the Americans or taking up skiing in his mid-50s, Jones had a prodigious appetite for achievement. One of those achievements was to have by-passed all sorts of Foreign Office assumptions about class, and all sorts of codebreakers' assumptions about the necessity of an Oxbridge education, to reach the pinnacle of decryption. He was an early emblem of what a classless meritocracy might look like.

Jerry Roberts

Of all the qualities said to run through the codebreakers, straightforward commercial acumen was not one of them. But Raymond Roberts – always known as Jerry – applied his quicksilver intellect to a post-war jet-age career of entrepreneurialism that took him across the Atlantic, and saw his market research companies working with the likes of Holiday Inn and Chrysler. That he was among the very few to have decrypted and read messages sent by Hitler himself was a satisfaction he had to enjoy in complete silence.

There were darker recollections too, though. When first pulled into Bletchley Park, in the early 1940s, Roberts had been on the team that was working on the 'Double Playfair' hand cyphers that were used by the Nazi military police. There were messages boasting of the obscene numbers of Jewish people that were being killed. Roberts and his fellow codebreakers were opening a window on the Holocaust.

That post-war career of buccaneering enterprise, unusual at a time when business and industry seemed calcified between time-serving management and time-serving shop floor, perhaps also suggested that there was an ever observant and restless individualism in Roberts. Whether breaking messages to reveal intelligence that would enable the Soviets to win the Battle of Kursk, or applying himself to the wonders of the Colossus machine, Roberts also took delight in reading the characters of his colleagues: from the industrial chemist Bill Tutte, staring into space and sucking a pencil in

left: Sarah Baring, then Norton, with her husband William Waldorf Astor, later 3rd Viscount Astor, during the 1945 General Election campaign, when he was standing as a Conservative candidate.
Evening Standard/ Getty Images

right: Osla Benning (left) attends the Whaddon Chase point-to-point near Bletchley with Babette Talbot Baines in March 1939.
Fox Photos/Getty Images

left: The Comtesse Maxime de la Falaise in a fashion shoot in 1951.
Walter Carone, Paris Match/Getty Images

right: Two master chess men and cryptographers: Harry Golombek plays Stuart Milner-Barry. *British Chess News*

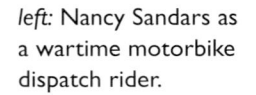

left: Nancy Sandars as a wartime motorbike dispatch rider.

right: Joan Clarke, once Alan Turing's fiancée, in 1945. *Agefotostock/Alamy*

above: The mural of Tommy Flowers on the wall of the eponymous pub in Poplar, East London.
Graham Coster

right: Asa Briggs in 1968, when Professor of History at the University of Sussex.
Fox Photos/Hulton Archive/Getty Images

left: Telford Taylor as US Chief Prosecutor at the lectern in 1947 during the Nuremberg Trials.
INTERSTOCK/ Alamy

left: Walter Eytan, then Israeli Ambassador to France, talking to General de Gaulle in 1969.
Keystone Press/ Alamy

left: The novelist Angus Wilson, photographed by Fay Godwin in 1974. *Alamy*

right: The avant-garde novelist Christine Brooke-Rose.

right: James Bernard, composer of the sinister soundtracks for the Dracula films as well as a friend of Benjamin Britten.

above: Dame Miriam Rothschild in her glasshouse at her home of Ashton Wold in 1991, together with a tawny owl.
John Glover/Alamy

right: The naturalist Duncan Poore in Glen Shiel in the Scottish Highlands he loved since schooldays.

left: Jane Fawcett: ballet dancer, opera singer and tireless campaigner to save St Pancras Station as well as Bletchley Park cryptographer.
Shaun Armstrong/Mubsta

left: Baroness Trumpington talking to Camilla Parker-Bowles, the Duchess of Cornwall, at the Southbank Centre in 2015.
Chris Jackson/Getty Images

above: Oliver and Sheila Lawn set about applying their wartime codebreaking skills to the mysterious 250-year-old coded inscriptions on the monuments at Shugborough Hall in Staffordshire.
PA Images/Alamy

left: Betty Webb makes the cover of *National Geographic* at the age of 92.

right: Jean Valentine at 82, reunited with one of the wartime Bombe machines she worked on, now fully restored and operational, on its unveiling at Bletchley Park.
PA Images/Alamy

left: Captain Jerry Roberts explains the working of a wartime codebreaking machine to Her Majesty the Queen during her visit to Bletchley Park in 2011.
PA Images/Alamy

abstraction, but seething with brilliant ideas; to the frustrated soldier and Home Secretary-to-be Roy Jenkins (see page 218), removed from the field to work in intelligence. This was true of Captain Roberts too, personally uneasy about not 'fighting the good fight', as he put it, yet he understood that he was more useful to the war at the Park. Immediately after VE Day, he was posted to Germany to join the War Crimes Investigations team, with which he stayed until 1947.

Born in Wembley in 1920, attending Latymer Upper School in Hammersmith, and spotted for Bletchley by his German professor at University College London, it might be said of Roberts that he was part of the post-war meritocracy, though he was rather more energetic and enterprising about his career than many of his peers. In later years, he also became a terrific advocate for the unsung successes of Tommy Flowers and Professor Max Newman to be recognised. In 2012 he was among the codebreaking veterans who guided the Queen around the restored Bletchley Park and its rebuilt machinery. Pleasingly, he was awarded the MBE the following year for 'services to codebreaking'.

THE NATURALISTS

Dame Miriam Rothschild

A formidable scientist and naturalist – to say nothing of a world expert on fleas – Dame Miriam Rothschild had poetry flowing through her veins as well as an all-consuming curiosity. 'I am incurably romantic,' she once said, 'hankering after small stars spangling the grass.'

Her academic achievements – doctorates, books – largely came about through her tenacious self-education (born in 1908, she entered a world in which brilliantly clever girls did not have anything like the same access to universities as their male siblings). As well as being recruited to Bletchley Park during the war, she was also intensely useful to the government because of her knowledge of parasites: it needed her research on how wood pigeons spread TB to cattle.

Dame Miriam, the grand-daughter of Lord Rothschild, was actually brought up quite close to Bletchley, in a house called Ashton Wold at the foot of the Chilterns. Her life was soon suffused with her passion for nature: as well as that pioneering study of fleas (a catalogue that took 30 years to amass), she was an evangelist for wildflowers and butterflies at a time between the wars when nature was taken for granted and consequently seriously threatened.

In 1939 she was among the first cohort to be recruited for the Park. Her chief role was that of a linguist, poring over intercepted messages from across Europe. In its earliest days, before its huge successes led to vast expansion, the Bletchley operation was still something of a cottage industry, and around the grounds, Dame Miriam's eye would not have missed a single moth or wildflower.

When not at Bletchley Park, Dame Miriam was sometimes found back at Ashton Wold playing host to some distinguished American servicemen. Clark Gable, she recalled, once dropped by for an afternoon's shooting. She was taken by how handsome he was, but confided that he appeared to be entirely lacking in a sense of humour.

After the war, her extraordinary career in natural science enjoyed a colourful efflorescence: trusteeship of the Natural History Museum, a hundred prizes and medals from the Royal Horticultural Society, plus the assignment from the Prince of Wales to transform his garden at Highgrove into a safe haven for rare species and wildflowers. Nor was her work on fleas simply esoteric academia: it was hugely important in terms of understanding chains of life (as well as providing fascinating asides, such as the gravitational pressure exerted on a flea when it jumped being roughly 29 times that of an Apollo astronaut blasting off for the Moon).

Peter Twinn

He was the man who, in the early months of 1940, had the honour of being the first to break into a live Enigma message, but thereafter Peter Twinn was enduringly modest about it. He was one of a small cohort, including Alan Turing, who had been shrewdly recruited before war broke out. Born in south London in 1916, and educated at Dulwich College and Brasenose College, Oxford, Peter Twinn was embarking upon a postgraduate mathematics course when an intriguing notice circulating around the university caught his eye. The government was looking for mathematicians, but no job description of any kind was given.

By the summer of 1939, Bletchley Park had been acquired, and senior codebreaker Alfred 'Dilly' Knox had set up his department in an outbuilding referred to as the Cottage. Twinn's training amounted to five minutes' examination of an old Enigma machine, and then his mercurial boss told him to get on with it.

He and Turing and Gordon Welchman did so with aplomb. While codebreaking had been by tradition a realm for classicists – ease and familiarity with decrypting ancient papyri and dead languages – this was now the age of the mathematicians. It was said that Alan Turing developed something of a crush on Twinn; Twinn, with sensitivity and good humour, rebuffed him. His early success in unpicking an Enigma setting was only the start; he went on to play an important role in the fight against the Naval ciphers.

The post-war years brought an intriguing variety of work. In the 1960s he was at the Ministry of Technology, heading up the development of hovercrafts (those who endured those rather seasicky journeys across the Channel in the 1970s would not have much to thank him for). But he was also a pioneering environmentalist. In the early 1970s he became secretary of the Natural Environment Research Council, at a time when 'the ecology' was very much a fringe concern. Twinn was among those determined to change that. He also diversified into entymology, eventually producing a book, *A Provisional Atlas of the Longhorn Beetle of Britain*, which became the last word on the subject.

Duncan Poore

There were a few for whom the codebreaking life seemed, weirdly, to dovetail rather beautifully with their own particular passions. The pioneering conservationist Duncan Poore, who travelled the world and studied everything from the delicate ecosystems of tropical rainforests to the windswept mountains of Scotland, was one of those Bletchley Park recruits who was sent voyaging across the world to HMS Anderson in Ceylon to work on Japanese codes.

The backdrop of that particular outstation was ludicrously rich in incredible wildlife. It is possible that it helped to change the direction of Poore's working life. Before Bletchley called, he had been studying Classics at Cambridge; after he was demobilised, he returned, but switched to Natural Sciences, with a particular focus on botany.

Poore, born in 1925, had been sent to the then dour Scottish school Glenalmond, in the foothills of the Highlands; he never lost his love of the heathery, mossy terrain. He was studying at Cambridge when the Bletchley Park spotters alighted upon him. Working on Japanese codes was a formidable proposition, as indeed was the prospect of the hazardous voyage to the Far East.

But something in that emerald landscape around the hills of Colombo clearly resonated. After pioneering work at Cambridge using aerial photography to study fenland wildlife, Poore moved to the University of Malaya, where his studies of the rainforests took over. During his career he also accepted an offer to be a lecturer at Oxford University, later becoming a professor, with particular interest in forestry. Poore worked closely with UNESCO and in 2003 published a book about the lives of forests, and how to manage them, called *Changing Landscapes*. Like many Bletchley alumni, Poore had a lateral intellect, in his case using to address the increasingly urgent question of how far we are taking for granted the natural world.

FORTUNES FAR AFIELD

Aileen Clayton

Codebreaking was a worldwide operation, and Aileen Clayton, as a Women's Auxiliary Air Force volunteer, took a pioneering role, being sent to Egypt in 1941 to help establish a super-efficient 'Y' (or 'wireless') service. Very soon, as the war intensified in the Mediterranean theatre, she insisted that she and her team of wireless interceptors be allowed to operate as close to the conflict as possible. Not only was this unusual for decryption/intelligence officers; it was also doubly unusual for women. But Clayton was indefatigable, and signals intelligence was a powerful tool in the fightback against Rommel's forces. As Aileen Clayton manoeuvred her way around north Africa, the jeopardy never let up; but neither did the quantities of invaluable intelligence flowing through her unit and back across the sea to Bletchley Park.

This is not to say that she was universally welcomed: she recalled the shock of male officers as she arrived in positions near the front, and the frequency with which she was told they had no accommodation available for women. Yet she was implacable and was always finally accepted. Sexism sometimes came in other forms: while she was in Cairo, she was dragooned into being soothing company (in an innocent way) for pilots on leave, sometimes taking them to bars or clubs, on the basis that a woman was able to bring comfort. One man, she remembered, very specifically wanted to take tea with her, out of proper china cups. He was later shot out of the sky. His parents wrote to Clayton afterwards thanking her for her friendship.

Fortunes Far Afield

One of the more harrowing episodes of her spectacular war career was in 1942 when she was on Malta, facing, like the rest of the population, what seemed like apocalyptic bombardment. She was yards away when a plane exploded on a runway; her jaw was broken by shrapnel. Nothing, though, was allowed to interrupt the flow of the decrypted intelligence.

Yet there were moments in wireless interception when operatives were confronted with the terrible deaths of the enemy. Before her Mediterranean postings, Clayton had been in English coastal stations, eavesdropping on German pilots who – assuming that they were being overheard – used to croon sentiments such as: 'Would you like me to drop a bomb on you? Whee- boom!' On one occasion, the RAF were able to get a very swift fix on the incoming danger, and it was Clayton, at her earphones, who could hear as the bullets tore into the plane, and the pilot went screaming to his death. She was forced to go outside to quell the nausea.

Hers was a role requiring speed and dexterity as well as lightning intelligence: from Benghazi to Algiers, Clayton and her colleagues were intercepting real-time encrypted messages, and without figures like her, Bletchley Park would not have had the broader harvest of clear, raw intelligence that enabled it to build up its own (analogue, card-index) database of the German war machine.

Jean Valentine

There are a few people who have the gift of holding an audience. They ascend the stage, simply start talking, and the audience is in their thrall. Jean Valentine, who was rather diminutive in stature, nevertheless had the knack of becoming the undivided focus of the room. She was a gifted and witty orator who, speaking without notes, once reduced His Royal Highness the Prince of Wales to fits of laughter.

These audiences came to her rather late in life, when she was in her mid-eighties. But no-one ever noticed her age; instead they saw her energy and sly comic timing. All of her force came from the extraordinary events of her youth that had moulded her life. She was living history.

Everyone grew up fast in the war, not least the teenage girls who were swept into wholly unexpected new lives, from steel smelting to rocket testing. But not every teenage girl was told by her parents that it was her absolute duty to set sail across U-boat-infested oceans to a top-secret base on another continent to carry out work, the nature of which they had no idea. This, though, was the experience of Jean Valentine, aged just 19 when she embarked upon the voyage, and the decryption role, that were to change her life.

Born in Perth, Scotland, in 1925, Jean was caught in Bletchley's gravitational pull as soon as she joined the Wrens in 1944 thanks to her mercurial intelligence and her addiction to cryptic crosswords. She was one of the young women co-opted – among other jobs – to tend to the mighty 'Bombe' combination crunching machines.

Fortunes Far Afield

Very shortly afterwards, her name went up on a board as one of those selected for Bletchley's overseas operations: she would be sent to Colombo, in what was then Ceylon. For this she needed written permission from her parents. And it was her father who, rather than pleading with his only child not to leave these shores, declared instead that it was her solemn duty to. What followed was a harrowing six-week voyage, bristling with jeopardy – and then her introduction to a world of intense colour and vivid experience.

She and her colleagues were working on Japanese codes; frequently, on night shifts in a silent, bamboo-walled office, Jean would find herself being interrupted by vast flying insects or snakes. She was immensely practical about removing them. By contrast to wartime Perth – a city of solemn grey – she now moved through a land drenched in colour and heat, enjoying sophisticated dances at smart hotels, taking trips out into the country to tea plantations.

But the work was intense: the range of Japanese messages was vast and of huge strategic importance. This also meant, though, that the job could bring great satisfaction and pride, especially to a teenager who had previously rarely left the Tay valley. It was while in this part of the world that she met her husband-to-be, then a pilot. When the war ended, they came back to London, but in the cold austerity of that time, it was unendurable, and they returned east.

Many years later when Bletchley Park itself had been restored and thrown open to the public, Jean Valentine embarked upon a new career, giving wholly unscripted talks about the codebreaking life. She was invited to St James's Palace to address the Prince of Wales; she had the chance to explain the workings of the Bombes to the Queen. When VIPs wanted to see the restoration of Bletchley Park, it was Jean Valentine they wished to show them around. Her sad death in 2019 – she was 94 years old – extinguished one of the most original lights of Bletchley Park, a figure from its past who worked tirelessly for its future.

Sheila Mackenzie

Although she knew nothing of the existence of a dedicated codebreaking operation, Sheila MacKenzie, who was studying Modern Languages at Aberdeen as war engulfed the world, knew she wanted to do as much as she could to help defeat Hitler. She was on a list 'reserved as a future teacher', but her frustration led her to remove her name. Shortly afterwards, she was asked down to London for interview by the Foreign Office. Then 'I got another letter, asking me to report to Bletchley.'

The work was gruelling, rather than glamorous: translation and decryption of messages intercepted from 'gun emplacements along the Dutch, Belgian and French coasts', for instance. 'You were translating German decrypts. And you really got to know how to do them pretty quickly . . . Night-watches were hell.'

And yet the self-enclosed world of Bletchley had its own allure. It was here that Sheila met her husband-to-be and fellow codebreaker Oliver Lawn; free summer days were spent exploring the countryside on her bicycle that she had called Griselda; free summer evenings saw her and Oliver throw themselves into their mutual passion for Highland dancing under the auspices of Hugh Foss. Her numerous billets, with local families of modest means, forged unexpected friendships.

Even amid the discipline and the rigour of this vital wartime work, life had an unforgettable texture and depth. Sheila MacKenzie was part of a rising generation of young women who knew they wanted — and deserved — a great deal more than the role of keeping house and raising family. And although Bletchley Park could never be spoken of, the work was nonetheless a vast achievement she could never lose touch with.

Following the war, she was determined that her intellectual life should not slide into abeyance. An original plan to teach in central Europe was thwarted by the clangour of the Iron Curtain dropping down, but she continued her studies in Britain, with a post-graduate focus on sociology. Eventually she and her husband retired to the wild, windy moors on the fringe of Sheffield, but the opening up of Bletchley's secrets suddenly brought Sheila and Oliver into almost constant demand from television stations and institutes wanting their expertise on esoteric matters.

Mimi Galilee

For most people in England in the post-war years, America was a sort of dream-realm; cinemas were the portal through which this young, colourful and abundant land was viewed. But there were a few British women and men who were determined to experience it first-hand, at a point when transatlantic flights were still largely a pre-jet-set fantasy.

One such was a young woman called Mimi Galilee who, rather strikingly, set out for New York City alone. Although she did not stay too long, the move fitted a pattern of determination and adventurousness. Later, she also had some years with the BBC World Service. Perhaps what had given Mimi Galilee a spur was her earlier secret life.

She was the youngest recruit to Bletchley Park, aged just 14 years old. And though her first role was that of messenger, hurrying between huts bearing documents of the utmost secrecy, she stayed on a little after the war, immersing herself deeper in the codebreaking world. What made Mimi Galilee's memories of the establishment so wonderful is that she brought an entirely novel – and beguiling perspective – to the 'wondrous beings', as she put it, who peopled those huts. In a sense, as an unmathematical teenager, she had more of an everyman view of a bewilderingly esoteric world.

Brought up in Stoke Newington, north London, Mimi and her sister were evacuated with their mother to the town of Bletchley. Mimi, who was very bright, enrolled in the local school but loathed it, and since in those days it was possible to leave young, she did, opting for a local job in an establishment that had been the source of ceaseless speculation among townsfolk. Mimi's mother had already found herself a wartime job as a cook in the codebreaking canteen; Mimi was interviewed by the fierce (though fair) personnel manager Doris Reid, and brought in as a messenger.

To her, the clever young graduates and sophisticated posh women who populated this teeming community of huts and grand house were 'like gods'. As well as Alan Turing and the intimidatingly 'bear-like' Josh Cooper, there were the breathtakingly glamorous women too. Mimi recalled the actress Dorothy Hyson, who had a chinchilla fur coat that made many other women 'groan' with envy.

As a messenger, she had unique freedom to move around and observe this strictly compartmentalised world; as a teenager, she felt the awesome weight of the Official Secrets Act on her (though, like other recruits, she never had any idea of what would actually happen if she did inadvertently give the secret away).

As time went on, and as a reward for youthful diligence, she was moved to other duties within the main directorate in the big house itself, witnessing first-hand the unique strains (but charmingly maintained manners) of Commander Edward Travis and figures such as Nigel de Grey. Thus, she was allowed to see what not even the highest-ranking MI6 intelligence agents were allowed to glimpse: the heart of the nation's gravest wartime secret.

As Bletchley was closed up in 1945, and the new codebreaking operation moved to Eastcote in north-west London, Mimi opted to stay in this world for a little longer; even though she knew she could never speak of it, the experience was still immersive. Eventually, she struck out: heading first to the US (quite a move then for a young single woman), and then returning some years later to work for the BBC World Service. It was within those corridors that she started to bump into old Bletchley faces. The mutual recognition was a shock of delight, but nothing could be said, even in private conversations, about their old lives.

HISTORIANS AND ARCHAEOLOGISTS

Mavis Lever

If there was a thread that ran through the varied career of Mavis Lever, it was a taste for intellectual adventure. She was born in south London in 1921, but there were few other schoolgirls of her generation who would have insisted that the family take its summer holiday in the Rhineland to celebrate her German O-level. After the war, when the fashion was for modernisation and renewal, again, few stuck out like Mavis Lever when it came to ensuring that treasured landscapes and historic gardens gained proper protection.

And at Bletchley, aged 19, it was her refusal to be stymied by the Italian Enigma codes that in 1941 led her to make the breakthrough that resulted in the British winning the Battle of Cape Matapan. Several years later, her work on the Abwehr codes ensured that the D-Day 'Double Cross' operation came off. Mavis Lever was a linguist, an aesthete and a ruthless logician; in itself quite an unusual combination.

She was recruited into Bletchley's 'Cottage' (having studied German Romantic poetry) under the formidably eccentric Dilly Knox. With no training, she launched herself into the cerebral challenges with gusto – and sometimes round the clock – having imagined, before she arrived, that she would be a glamorous Mata Hari-style secret agent but concluding that she 'didn't have the legs'.

It was at Bletchley that she met and fell in love with Keith Batey and, as was frequently the case after the war, the intensity of Bletchley was replaced by the role of home maker. This could not last. By the 1960s, she was leading the way in the relatively new field of landscape history. As well as writing books, she campaigned for the preservation of 'Parks and Gardens of Special Interest', eventually becoming among other things a driving force in the National Heritage Memorial Fund.

When at last the Bletchley secret was disclosed, Mavis Batey never downplayed her achievements, but left it to others to marvel at the idea of a teenage girl in the hidebound 1940s taking such an active lead.

Harry Hinsley

One of the curiosities of Bletchley was that it was sometimes its youngest recruits that were in the driving seat of history. One such young man, at the age of 25, found himself undergoing something like a 36-hour shift in June 1944 as D-Day unfolded; his responsibility was to relay, instantly, intelligence procured from encrypted German communications. This was one of the means – enabling anticipation of enemy moves – by which the Allies could evade being forced back into the sea.

By this stage in his codebreaking career, Harry Hinsley was regarded by his superiors as something of a genius. Even as a beginner, he had a nose for detecting anomalies in encrypted messages that helped in their speedy unravelling and analysis. And like many other young recruits, he did not hail from a grand public school background; rather, his father was an ironworks waggoner in the Midlands. Hinsley, born in 1918, had attended the Walsall Grammar School. From there he was catapulted by the force of his intellect into St John's College, Cambridge: his field, history. He was part way through his course when war broke out, and he found himself on the cross-country railway from Oxford to Bletchley.

After his codebreaking war – years of expert German wireless traffic analysis, and hunch-following – he returned to St John's to pick up where he had left off. If he missed the intensity of Bletchley at all, he found his own highly focused pitch, almost hypnotising grateful students with brilliant lectures and tutorials. There was a constant sense of jeopardy in his rooms that came with the possibility of being crushed under an avalanche of the books crammed madly into all available shelves and corners.

In the 1970s Hinsley, an expert in international relations, was called upon to revisit the old days discreetly with a history of *British Intelligence in the Second World War*. Bletchley was still half in the shadows of official secrets, making this task a masterclass in nuance and subtlety (especially since he also had to deal with the views and criticisms of other governments and their own secrecy sensitivities when responding to advance view of the manuscript). What this academic work could not convey was the warm atmosphere of the Park even in dark days: Hinsley had met his wife-to-be – another codebreaker called Hilary Brett-Smith – in among those huts.

Asa Briggs

One of the abiding assumptions made of the immediate post-war period was that windows of opportunity opened wide for grammar school-educated boys from the provinces. These assumptions are not always wrong. Asa Briggs, Yorkshire-born and educated in Keighley, was to achieve as much academic and public prominence as anyone from the more privileged public schools. What is more, he would be responsible for spreading all that knowledge wider still. In addition, he was a prolific historian and author, part of a new generation of men and women who rose during the 'white heat' of Harold Wilson's government. Asa – later Lord – Briggs was by the 1970s one of the great public intellectuals. He was also among those who, decades beforehand, had been pulled into Bletchley Park's web more by serendipity than mathematical skill.

Asa Briggs had precociously studied History and Economics at Sidney Sussex College, Cambridge aged 16, and found himself receiving the slightly unexpected summons to the Park in 1942. The invitation to Station X arose not out of his academic disciplines, but from his talent for chess: at Cambridge, he had played with Howard Smith – a mathematician who would decades later become head of MI5. Smith had himself been drawn into the Bletchley vortex, recalled Briggs, and recommended him to Gordon Welchman.

The twenty-one-year-old Briggs found himself in Hut 6 and, as befitted the spirit of the forthcoming age, was cheered and impressed by what he saw as an essence of equality in the way the Park worked: that when it came to offering ideas and suggestions, there was no feeling that lower ranks had to hold back, or indeed would be held back. There was, it seemed, only one person at the time who appeared to command a sort of silent deference, and that was Alan Turing – a tribute to his genius rather than his bearing.

Although this was not an atmosphere of uniforms or drills, Asa Briggs was classed as an intelligence officer: this title came with a peaked cap and a reasonable salary. But that sense of equality – even among the debs – he loved at Bletchley was a principle he carried firmly into Attlee's post-war world. As well as academic appointments to Worcester College, Oxford and the University of Leeds, Briggs was, in the 1960s, with Jennie Lee, one of the driving forces behind the Labour government's more egalitarian creations, the Open University. Around the same time he was also one of the founding fathers of the new University of Sussex. This brought further education within reach of those who would never before have thought they had a chance.

His great passion was for the spread of knowledge: his history books – such as his social history trilogy on *Victorian Cities*, *Victorian People* and *Victorian Things* – had a note of social optimism, and were popular as well as academically lauded.

Lord Briggs also had a Zelig-like ability to move among, and influence, some of the era's most extraordinary figures. He tutored a young newspaper-magnate-to-be: Rupert Murdoch. The pair even made a field trip to the Middle East. And he was a frequent visitor to Mao's China, at a time when the left was perhaps a little more naïve about the depth and the scale of the human catastrophe he had presided over.

At Bletchley, Asa Briggs had been required to stay silent about all he had seen and learned. In his post-war life, he more than made up for this, through books, the television and at the lectern.

And as an avatar of a new more socially concerned society, his recruitment to the Park was a sign of the social reordering of the nation that was to come.

Jane Fawcett

As a jewel of Victorian Gothic, festooned with rich detailing, the restored St Pancras Station with its grand station hotel is widely adored. A century later the new-build British Library next door politely echoed its red bricks – but it might never have had the opportunity. It is always startling to think that in the late 1960s St Pancras's quirky feast of arches and turrets was just inches away from being demolished and replaced by a modernist box. At a time when nineteenth-century architecture was regarded as lethally reactionary in a new world of planned towns and shopping precincts, one of those with the vision to campaign for the old station was Jane Fawcett, a key figure in the Victorian Society. She – alongside John Betjeman – was among the very few who knew instinctively that future generations would adore the original grandeur of St Pancras.

That combination of a sharp aesthetic sense and an equally sharp eye for human potential informed her wide-ranging career. Before the war, Jane Fawcett (née Hughes) had been a trained ballerina, taught by Ninette de Valois at Sadler's Wells. She had attended studio sessions with Margaret Fonteyn. While acting had been her first choice of career – she had actually won a scholarship to the Royal Academy of Dramatic Art – dance became her passion. But her ruthless tutors told her that her 'back was too long' and she 'was too tall', and would have no future in ballet.

Such a free spirit could not be smothered so easily. Jane had already succeeded in breaking free of the conventions of smart society that had sent her as a girl to be prepared for 'the Season' at a 'school for young ladies' that considered examinations and university degrees as most unsuitable for those of a certain background. In the late 1930s she was even sent to learn German in Switzerland. It was this, together with the general trustworthiness of debutantes, that drew her into Bletchley Park's orbit.

The senior hierarchy there soon had reason to be grateful. It was Jane's close attention to the screed of apparent gibberish she was typing into a decoding machine that mimicked the German Enigma code that enabled her to see the faintest echoes of the message emerging. At the time the hunt was on for the German battleship *Bismarck*: Jane realised the message she was handling suggested it was heading for Brest, on the French coast. She was absolutely right, and the sinking of the *Bismarck* was a brilliant coup both militarily and in terms of national morale. Naturally the source of the intelligence had to be kept invisible.

Yet Jane Fawcett did not find Bletchley a congenial place to live. Walking along the dim path that led to the Park entrance to report for night shifts, she always carried a brick in her handbag: 'You never knew who you might meet,' she remarked crisply.

Whereas for some the post-war aftermath of the intense Bletchley life was an anti-climax, Jane Fawcett had no trouble in finding new avenues to explore. After marrying naval officer Ted Fawcett, she enrolled at the Royal Academy of Music to pursue a career in singing, while at the same time bringing up their two small children. Becoming a professional opera singer, she performed a variety of roles in everything from *Der Rosenkavalier* to *Le Nozze di Figaro*. But as the children grew older she became reluctant to let the demands of touring part her from her family.

Instead, by the 1960s her volcanic energies were channelled into the Victorian Society. With Britain's nineteenth-century architectural legacy being torn down in cities and towns in favour of

Historians and Archaeologists

Communistic brutalism (see the entire centre of Birmingham), powerful voices were needed to save elegant landmarks. In the case of St Pancras, the British Rail hierarchy came to refer to her as 'the furious Mrs Fawcett'. Later she became a fellow of the Royal Institute of British Architects. She only returned to Bletchley Park in 2009, out of curiosity to see once more the rather unlovely house which one of her own students at RIBA had been instrumental in saving.

Nancy Sandars

Cuneiform tablets and cave paintings are, in their own ways, cryptograms: literature and art that require intelligence and sensitivity to unlock their meanings. Nancy Sandars brought a singular intellect to her archaeological work that was instrumental in enabling people to look at artefacts in a wholly new way. Whereas previous generations had been accustomed to interpreting the Lascaux cave paintings in primitive religious terms, Sandars made a plea for them as pure joyous representative art for its own sake. In the course of her career she also translated *The Epic of Gilgamesh* for Penguin; her version went on to sell over a million copies. During the war, Sandars applied her intelligence to the business of German radio intercepts in the Y Service, gathering, decrypting and translating – at lightning speed – the communications between Luftwaffe pilots and their controllers.

For someone so totally immersed in the ancient darkness of the past – her archaeological career began in the 1930s – Nancy Sandars, born in Oxfordshire in 1914, was also very active and well-travelled, having experienced Spain and Germany as the shadows of fascism lengthened. When war came she was a motorbike dispatch rider, an incredibly demanding job involving round-the-clock journeys, sometimes in lethal conditions. Once, during a storm, her bike's engine failed and delivered an electric shock that sent her skidding off the road to end up pinned beneath the machine.

But her time in the Y-Service, in small coastal listening stations from Cornwall to Kent, was no less hazardous. The Luftwaffe pilots had a good idea where these listening posts were housed, and frequently swooped to strafe them. Yet here too was the strange, queasy intimacy of the Bletchley Y operation: those secret listeners came to know some of those enemy pilots above via the rhythms and style of their language. And they heard their death cries when they were shot out of the sky.

The post-war years, starting at St Hugh's College, Oxford, brought a flowering of academic achievement, and archaeological projects that took her from the Middle East to deep behind the Iron Curtain. She also wrote books, including *Prehistoric Art in Europe*, and pursued an intense fascination with the 'sea-peoples': Mediterranean sea raiders of the twelfth century. Hers was an encompassing passion: the ancient forgotten treasures beneath the soil, allied to an aliveness to ancient poetry and art that conjured different worlds.

In the mid-1980s she was made a fellow of the Royal Academy of Arts. She returned to the old family home in Oxfordshire, not far from the prehistoric Rollright Stones. How strange and fleeting those Morse messages captured from the wartime air – sometimes triumphant, sometimes despairing – must by then have seemed.

Stuart Staveley

If one was to be talent-spotted by anyone, who better than Ian Fleming, the creator of James Bond? Fleming, who served in Naval Intelligence throughout the war, and was one of the few figures outside the Park to know precisely what was going on inside it, had interviewed a new naval recruit who had just recently won a place at Queen's College, Oxford. Stuart Staveley, born in Birkenhead in 1926 and entering the conflict mid-war, had been reading Ancient History. Perhaps it was this propensity for deciphering extinct languages that registered with Fleming. But Staveley had another passion which, in its layers of cunning and guile and mental mathematical acumen, would also have commended him to the authorities: the game of bridge.

Staveley was told to present himself at an odd, secret, requisitioned classroom above the gas showroom on Bedford Broadway just a few miles from Bletchley Park, and it was from here that he was inducted into the complexities of the Japanese language, and the Japanese encryption system.

He picked up his studies of Ancient History after the war, gaining his doctorate and becoming a lecturer at St Andrews and then the University of London. Staveley was also a keen chorister, like so many of the other codebreakers, he had sung with the Liverpool Philharmonic and found romance and marriage at an opera society. Soon he and his wife formed the English Bridge Union, an organisation that was connected nationally and internationally with bridge societies and competitions the world over. The passion was clearly shared: membership multiplied again and again, and Staveley was an invaluable source of news and intelligence for newspaper and magazine bridge correspondents. Ian Fleming's Bond was an individualist in his card tastes; bridge is about subtlety and team work, which is why Bond could never have been an effective codebreaker, whereas Staveley was.

Lord Dacre Of Glanton

There are professional catastrophes that can make even enemies wince. One such was suffered by the highly distinguished historian Lord Dacre of Glanton in the 1980s. He had been called upon by the *Sunday Times* to examine, and authenticate, a set of diaries. These were allegedly the very diaries kept by Adolf Hitler. As a historical discovery, it was – if authentic – extraordinary and significant.

Lord Dacre – better known as Hugh Trevor-Roper – had specialised insight: in November 1945 he had been sent into Berlin as part of an intelligence operation to piece together the still hazy details of Hitler's last days. Stalin, for his own unknowable reasons, was encouraging rumours that Hitler and Eva Braun had escaped alive. Trevor Roper's job was to prove his death – for how else could the defeated and de-Nazified German population find peace if there was an inkling that the Führer might yet return? That was the thinking, though there was scant evidence that many of them would have been thrilled to see him back.

That mission took him down to the darkness of Hitler's bunker and deep into Germany's forests, rounding up and interrogating various courtiers who had gone to ground, while also revelling in the landscape and the crisp, refreshing wines, in an effort to stop the Soviets controlling the currents of history. It also produced a bestselling book, *The Last Days of Hitler*, that is still in print today.

Historians and Archaeologists

Trevor-Roper was informed of the provenance of these newly 'discovered' Hitler diaries by journalists, and he did not have the luxury of time for doubt, as the newspaper was ticking towards deadline. But he was also a director on the board of *The Times*, and knew that it and its sister paper were not usually given to chasing sensationalism. He told the *Sunday Times* that the diaries were most probably genuine. Alas, a fortnight later, the diaries were revealed to be a very intricate hoax.

Given that Hugh Trevor-Roper had exulted in venomous academic feuds throughout his career, the resulting *Schadenfreude* was intense, yet there was also an element of agonised sympathy. It was not needed: Trevor-Roper was sufficiently witty to take care of himself.

Interestingly, even in 1983, when this debacle occurred, little was known of Trevor-Roper's deeper wartime intelligence experience. Then again, nothing in his quiet, bookish Northumbrian childhood – born the son of a country doctor in 1914 – or in his education at Charterhouse, then Christ Church, Oxford, could have suggested the firebrand codebreaking maverick he would become. Recruited from Oxford for the Radio Security Service, an intelligence cousin of Bletchley monitoring enemy transmissions, he found himself first working in a cell in Wormwood Scrubs prison. (The actual prisoners had been evacuated to farther-flung jails in case of bombing). Trevor-Roper was focusing on Abwehr encryptions, and one night in his Ealing lodgings, he cracked them by hand.

The hierarchy at Bletchley were profoundly uncomfortable with Trevor-Roper stamping about on what they considered their territory. He, blithely unconcerned, persisted in unravelling German Abwehr (or secret service) codes as a contribution to counter-espionage against Nazi agents across Europe. But Trevor-Roper built up a terrific expertise that in the years that followed was reluctantly called upon by Bletchley, and he relished the chance to visit as he could indulge his love of hunting with the nearby Whaddon Hunt.

The Last Days of Hitler was a huge success, and Trevor Roper's subsequent academic career at Oxford was similarly colourful. He took a deep interest in the seventeenth century, on which he published a number of canonical works. In 1979 Mrs Thatcher's government made him a life peer, as Lord Dacre of Glanton, and the following year, at the age of 66, he moved across to Cambridge to become Master of Peterhouse, where he continued to act as an iconoclast, sending the Fellows into paroxysm of agitation. Those same enemies exulted in that awful 'Hitler Diaries' mistake. Worse still, the debacle overshadowed his wartime codebreaking work to the extent that few are even aware of it.

Joan Thirsk

Joan Thirsk was a historian who changed the way people looked not only at the past, but also at the landscape around them. At a time when the academic pursuit of history was largely focused on politics and battles and great men, she evangelised for a more profound immersion in the ordinary lives of those who had gone before.

Joan Thirsk (née Watkins, born in 1922) had a particular fascination for the agricultural history of early modern England: the communities who worked the land, and how they worked it, particularly through times of national trauma, such as the Black Death or the famines of the Tudor years. There was a new kind of intellectual rigour here that demanded a much broader selection of primary sources. In a sense, from the Reformation to the repercussions of the Civil War, she was summoning ghosts, enabling her readers not only to understand the complexities of agriculture, but also see what people were eating, and drinking, and wearing, and very often to explore the role of women within these historical rural communities.

This blend of intellect and empathy might have been developed by Joan Thirsk's early gift for languages, shaped at the Camden School for Girls: another form of portal into different lives and thinking. It was this that brought her to Bletchley Park, and in the decryptions and especially in the intricate cross-referencing of decoded messages, Joan Thirsk also came to understand how one may create a detailed picture of the world outside by intelligently putting these sources together. This was not the only felicitous conjunction at Bletchley, for it was at the Park that she met her husband-to-be, Jimmy.

Her early academic career after the war – she had been studying at the University of London – took her to the University of Leicester (Senior Research Fellow in Agrarian History) and thence to Oxford. Her pioneering book in the late 1950s was *English Peasant Farming: The Agrarian History of Lincolnshire*. Subsequent titles delved into food, and the development of consumer society. She was a member of the Royal Commission on Historic Monuments, and in the early 1990s was awarded the CBE. Bletchley Park may have played a part in her intellectual evolution, but the life beyond it was even more fulfilling.

Professor John Evans

In some ways, archaeologists create visions of worlds: by deciphering hieroglyphs and ancient art and pottery and sculpture, they summon vivid and colourful images of distant, alien and yet somehow also immediate civilisations. Professor John Evans, who was brought into Bletchley Park a little later in the war, by which time it was a hyper-efficient codebreaking factory, might have applied some of that talent for detailed visualisation and interpretation to his work on Enigma code settings. The career he pursued afterwards above all required imaginative empathy: to dig deep into the past, to analyse bones and fragments, and from these to see living, breathing, thinking people was more than just a talent. He was also one of the first to popularise this kind of work on television.

Born in Liverpool in 1925, Evans was a seriously bright child who won a scholarship to read English at Cambridge. The war interrupted what the Cambridge lecturer F. R. Leavis termed 'the Common Pursuit', and after it Evans seemed to have been seized with a deeper passion. He completed his English degree, but thereafter stayed on to plunge into the disciplines of anthropology and archaeology.

His focus was on ancient Mediterranean cultures, and particularly the prehistory of Malta. This growing expertise found gratitude on the island itself, as his excavations added enormously to the wealth of material at Valetta museum. It was out of this work that came a late 1950s BBC TV programme: a new sort of show that was a kind of precursor to Kenneth Clark's *Civilisation*. Evans plunged himself into a realm of prehistoric remnants and the vestiges of ancient temples. With this came new evidence and theories about how cultures flowered, how ideas spread, and what sort of ideas somehow remained in certain regions. How, he set about finding out, had early societies such as flourished on Malta moved from Neolithic subsistence farming to the construction of rich elaborate temples and catacombs?

By the 1970s, Professor Evans was heading up the Institute of Archaeology in London (as well as being made a Fellow of the Royal Academy, among many other distinctions). It would be a silly stretch to say he was a role model for Indiana Jones, yet his passionate advocacy for his discipline found it a wide and intrigued audience.

Felicity Ashbee

The great banks of futuristic machines with whirring drums and winking lights and treacherous fine sprays of oil would surely have been anathema to a true child of the Arts and Crafts movement. Equally, there would surely have been some discomfort among that woman's superiors at Bletchley Park about her uncompromising communism.

Felicity Ashbee was in some lights one of the more unlikely recruits to codebreaking: her skills lay in pulsating art with a fierce social conscience. And she was acutely mindful of her family legacy. Her father was C. R. Ashbee, who had founded the Guild of Handicraft in London's Whitechapel in the twilight of the Victorian age. This Guild was an impassioned reaction to the coming of the machines: furniture makers, textile weavers, cabinet makers and stained-glass artists were drawn through its doors and would work diligently by hand, their very labour itself becoming a form of art. Felicity herself, who was born in the Cotswolds in 1913, was always aware of the purity of these ideals, and a great chronicler of the movement. Her book about her mother, *Janet Ashbee: Love, Marriage and the Arts and Craft Movement*, was a vivid depiction of an aesthetic demi-monde (Janet was a 'comrade wife' to the gay C. R. Ashbee).

In the 1930s, Felicity Ashbee trained at the Byam Shaw School of Art. The Spanish Civil War was the moment when her art and her politics fused: her anti-fascist posters carried genuine punch – one such fund-raising effort, featuring an emaciated child surrounded by upturned hands, featured the line: 'They face famine in Spain, They need clothes.'

When war came to Britain, she volunteered for the WAAF, and this in turn led her to that train journey from Euston Station. She remembered that Bletchley's authorities were wary of her staunch political stance, but there was some giddying success when she was the one who alerted her officers to the fact of Rudolf Hess's plane as it carried him on his mad mission to Scotland in 1941. In addition to this, she contributed enormously to the Park's artistic and theatrical life.

Art dominated her post-war life too, together with writing; hers was a world of tall-ceilinged, gaunt Kensington studios and a home in the then highly bohemian and down-at-heel Notting Hill. She became a formidable historian of art, and of art movements, writing books and academic journals and always safeguarding the memory of the ever-influential Arts and Crafts years.

Denis Twitchett

By throwing open doors into the past, and bringing fresh and new understanding of former empires, history can sometimes have a profound effect on the present, and on how diplomatic relations are conducted. For a very long time, the ancient – and distant – history of China was like dark matter to most people in the West: the nation's story was told largely through historic encounters involving Western travellers. And this had an effect on the way modern China was treated. But in a fast-modernising post-war world, this ignorance could not stand.

It is possible that it was his years at Bletchley Park that first inspired Professor Denis Twitchett to make a thorough and pioneering (in Western terms) exploration of Chinese history. He had done the Japanese crash course and worked on Japanese codes and set sail for HMS Anderson in Colombo. This in turn led him after the war to extend his academic career from Cambridge to Japan. And from there his fascination with those echoing gaps in our knowledge of Chinese history grew.

It was possibly also his experience of being confronted with seemingly impossible codes that gave Twitchett the intellectual confidence to study centuries-old Chinese documentation, and from these exquisite primary sources build up a detailed and colourful picture of the Tang Dynasty that had reigned some 1,300 years ago. His inquisitiveness ranged from ancient power struggles to the details of tax collection to the beauty of Tang music.

Twitchett also delved deep into the later Ming dynasty, again broadening understanding of a subject that had simply seemed obscure. He wrote books such as *Printing and Publishing in Medieval China*, was a valued contributor to *The Times Atlas of World History* and oversaw the multi-volume *Cambridge History of China*.

China, for many, still seems unknowable, but Professor Twitchett was brilliant at demonstrating that intellectual bridges could always foster greater mutual appreciation and understanding between great powers. To the ancient sources he studied must have been brought the same desire to understand that fuelled the patience required for the unravelling of wartime codes.

Jean Howard

There can be an intimacy about unravelling a code: as the true voice emerges, it is as if it is being silently, furtively, overheard. Jean Howard took this curious invisible closeness a stage further by following the encrypted messages of one particular man. They were separated by hundreds of miles, and he had no idea that his words were being laid naked before a young woman in Buckinghamshire. The man was Count László Almásy, a young man born of the Austro-Hungarian Empire who, as an explorer of the North African deserts, had offered his services to Rommel. Whether giving expert advice on the cartography of the sands, or suggesting ways in which the British advances might be thwarted, *Almásy* was endlessly sending enciphered dispatches to Rommel's HQ. And in Buckinghamshire, Jean Howard was analysing each and every one of them. Almásy was the partial inspiration for Michael Ondaatje's novel *The English Patient* and, all those decades after Bletchley Park, Jean Howard was consulted over the screenplay for the film adaptation starring Ralph Fiennes and Kristin Scott-Thomas.

This was just one episode of a whole career in intelligence. Yet Jean Howard entered the world of shadows by chance. She had initially volunteered as a nurse, and had been treating grievously wounded sailors up in the port of Grimsby. In these gritty surrounds she contracted scarlet fever and had to withdraw. She could not quite think where next to turn to aid the war effort, until she saw an advertisement asking for Italian and German interpreters. Jean

Howard had an ease with languages: she had been educated by a French governess, and sent to Germany and Austria by means of finishing school.

Born Jean Alington in 1917, she was the daughter of a vice-admiral, and held fast to that naval sense of duty. After answering the 'interpreter' advertisement, she was routed to Bletchley, landed in Hut 3, worked on German decrypts and before long was made a senior administrative officer.

Later in the war she threw herself into the maze that was Yugoslavian politics, and in particular the apparent riddle of why the British, and the Special Operations Executive, appeared to favour the claim to power made by the Communist Tito. Marriage to Major Roger Howard came in 1944, and after the war she pursued her keen interest in the stratagems of various branches of British intelligence, and their motives, for many more years. She was aware, through wide reading, how close she had been to the swirling tide of history and to those, like the curious figure of Almásy, who had been trying to shape its course. Release from such matters came, perhaps unsurprisingly given her naval upbringing, in the form of sailing.

JOURNALISTS AND BROADCASTERS

William Edward Crankshaw

Even the loftier realms of broadsheet journalism require its practitioners to be sharp, direct, fast and shrewd. Edward Crankshaw was a very familiar byline in the 1950s, especially to readers of the left-leaning *Observer*. But although he was writing for the duffel-coated Ban-The-Bomb intelligentsia, his own hinterland was a rather more complex mosaic. Crankshaw was interesting and passionate about Russia, at a time when the ever-frostier Cold War and the 1956 invasion of Hungary were making many re-evaluate their opinions of the Soviet Union. Yet he wrote with deep knowledge and experience; he was a reporter who had been involved with diplomacy and the Deep State to the most unusual degree. His wartime career had taught him the importance of interpretation, and of the possibility of misunderstood meaning.

As well as super-bright mathematicians, Bletchley Park also needed those who could read all the shades of human nature. Breaking the codes was only one part of the mighty worldwide operation: ensuring that the ensuing valuable intelligence was used wisely was another. At the start of the war, when the province of Ultra breakthroughs was kept secret even from senior military commanders, there was sometimes difficulty persuading them that this miraculous intelligence was true. From 1941, when Hitler declared war on Soviet Russia, making Joseph Stalin an unexpected ally of Britain, similar care had to be taken when feeding his forces intelligence. Edward Crankshaw, born in the genteel east London suburb of

Journalists and Broadcasters

Woodford, and subsequently a *Times* journalist, was the man sent to Moscow to act as liaison: an exquisite balancing act. His background was not mathematics, but literature, and an abiding fascination for Russia and its cruel history.

A posting to Moscow, while extraordinarily exciting, was also fraught: Major Crankshaw, as part of the Y-Service, was facing the daily unpredictability of a despot who had initiated mass killings and secret police terror without the flicker of an eyebrow. It was vital that the Red Army received the best of Bletchley's intelligence, yet it was also vital that they never guessed just how deeply into the Nazi codes the British had penetrated. As the tides of war changed, and the Red Army began decisively pushing the Nazis back, Crankshaw was eventually recalled from Moscow and given a rather more sedate posting back at Bletchley Park itself.

After the war, his literary and journalistic talents made him a familiar name. There were episodes of dark irony too. In the early 1950s, Crankshaw was summoned by the intelligence official Guy Burgess to be informed crossly that in his journalism he was being 'too soft' on Russia. It was not long afterwards that Burgess – one of the Cambridge Spies – defected. The double irony was that Burgess may have known nothing of Crankshaw's secret Y-Service war posting. The threads of intelligence frequently criss-crossed in arresting patterns.

Waldo Maguire

In 1964, while working out the tone and texture of Britain's forthcoming third television channel – which was to be known as BBC2 – the BBC's Editor of Television News made a revolutionary change. Instead of having the news read by trained actors and 'television personalities', as it still was on BBC1, the new channel would instead have bulletins hosted by 'working journalists'. As if this was not revolution enough, the Editor also decreed that some special bulletins would carry sign language for the deaf.

Several years later, this visionary was sent to be the BBC Controller in Northern Ireland, the land where he had been brought up. This was a position of acute sensitivity – and multiple dangers and hazards – as 'the Troubles' began to intensify. None the less, this man had an intellect (as well as gusto) that few around could match. Waldo Maguire was, for many of his colleagues, a source of wonder and amusement. None will have known what he did during the war. This, strikingly, included his wife Lilian – strikingly because she did the *same* thing during the war. They knew they were forbidden to discuss it with each other.

Born in 1920, and educated in Portadown, Magure attended Trinity College Dublin. He read Philosophy, but had a keen interest in both chess and mathematics. And the tendrils of Bletchley stretched far, even into neutral Ireland. Possibly because of the chess connection, Maguire worked for a time alongside that great genius of the game Harry Golombek.

Journalists and Broadcasters

Maguire's intellectual exuberance and wit made him a natural fit for the Park. But he also had an innate feel for the power of communication, and after the war this took him immediately into the BBC. At the time, the nascent television service was an inventive two-and-sixpence effort run and broadcast largely from Alexandra Palace in North London. Maguire was part of that generation of young talent who began to shape broadcasting into its more recognisable modern form: a BBC where the breadth of journalism, as well as the most scrupulous standards and ethics, was moulded. The BBC News that we – and the world – see today was in part conceived by Maguire and his colleagues.

The tensions of late 1960s/early 1970s Northern Ireland were if anything more stressful than anything he had ever faced in the war: threats from both sides, constant vigilance, fear for his family. Maguire had a stroke and eventually had to be eased away from his role. But his retirement, in the south of England, was filled with fishing and fuschia growing, and he and his wife lived long enough to see the veil of secrecy surrounding Bletchley finally torn away.

Anne Russell

Physicality was never really part of the codebreaking brief, but there were some recruits to the Park, like Anne Russell, who seethed with it. She was the daughter of an army officer, born in 1923 and brought up at Brayton Hall in Cumbria amid bracing vistas. Horses were central to family life. And Anne Lee (her maiden name), drawn to Bletchley as a cipher clerk, and working next door to Alan Turing, where she remembered seeing his tea mug affixed to the radiator with two padlocks to prevent theft, was fired with the zeal to fight the good fight. This meant that curiously Bletchley was not the most noteworthy period of her war.

That came a little later when, following D-Day in 1944, she got herself a job driving ambulances for the Free French Forces, reaching into Germany. This was a harrowing business: there were constant near-misses involving shells and bullets, and one astonishing cliffhanger when, driving pell-mell to get a casualty to suitable medical help, her ambulance drew into a German town that had yet to be entered by the Allies. She was awarded the Croix de Guerre.

All this only sharpened her appetite to see the just conclusion of the war. But her idealism led her into more ambiguous corners: in France, some of her closest comrades were preparing to head off for French Indo-China, and she was resolved to join them. She and others set sail for Saigon, her plan to continue with ambulance driving.

The French authorities, however, wanted to use her sharp wit in a rather more considered role. She was drafted into the French Intelligence Service – the Deuxième Bureau. There were stratagems involving her winning the trust of the Vietnamese rebels to glean information from them. But she came to believe there was some cause for them to act as they did. It thus became clear to her superiors that she was troubled by the ethics and morality of the conflict.

So Anne Russell returned to England, and found an eclectic career in journalism that ranged from interviewing Agatha Christie to becoming the assistant editor of a magazine called *Coal*, the in-house journal of the National Coal Board. If all of this lacked the visceral thrill of accelerating an ambulance through a barrage of rockets, or watching Alan Turing in action, it certainly had an attractive flavour of non-conformism.

LIFELONG CODEBREAKERS

Sir Edward Travis

For some, the war never ended; the conflict was simply re-focused, with new enemies and new technology. The man who was to shape Bletchley Park's post-war codebreaking future, moulding it into its regenerated form of GCHQ, was born in an era when Britain and Russia were engaged in their Great Game in Asia. He lived to see that game take on a whole new form, with America as the dominant partner facing the Soviets. Commander Edward Travis was the opposite of fusty; he was the man who gave Bletchley a rocket-blast of energy and his codebreakers dominion over the world's encryptions.

Travis, born in 1888 in south-east London (for quirky context, this was just weeks before Jack the Ripper began his murder spree in Whitechapel), was swift to join the Royal Navy immediately after leaving school in 1906. His predilection for cryptography was also revealed early: upon the outbreak of the Great War, he became signals officer to Admiral Jellicoe, and demonstrated the weakness of the admiral's own encryption system by breaking both it and its apparently more secure replacement.

By 1919, he was deputy to Alastair Denniston in the newly created Government Code and Cipher School, which was at first based in the rather swish avenue of Queen's Gate in South Kensington. With the Second World War looming, it was Travis who worked hard to devise a structure at Bletchley under which all three military services could have their codebreaking efforts co-ordinated (curiously, this was one of the weaknesses of their German counterparts, who kept services and departments separate, thus encouraging rivalry as opposed to co-operation).

And it was to Travis that ultimately the senior codebreakers and the head of MI6, Sir Stewart Menzies, turned in February 1942 when his boss Alastair Denniston was moved sideways. Travis, with a gruff manner and his nickname Jumbo, was a dynamic personality who inspired energy and confidence. His memos were written in brown ink. The codebreakers referred to this as 'the Director's Blood'. There was also a family element at the Park: one of his daughters, Valerie, came to work there. Travis also carefully oversaw the diplomatic delicacies of sharing codebreaking intelligence with the Americans; a feat pulled off with such aplomb that that particular alliance remains strong to this day. Administrative skill was one thing, but Travis also had a keen understanding of human nature, and of the foundations of trust.

The post-war years saw the establishment move out of Bletchley and into the Betjeman Metroland idyll of Eastcote: spooks amid the bowler-hatted commuters in their suburban villas. Though the number of codebreakers necessarily diminished, the new atomic landscape meant there could be not a moment of complacency. When Stalin tested his first nuclear bomb in Kazakhstan in 1949, the axis of world politics shifted. The freshly knighted Sir Edward Travis and his dedicated team – many veterans from the inter-war years – were under new, unfathomable pressures.

By 1952, the move from Eastcote to a new, purpose-built codebreaking centre at Cheltenham was imminent, and at the age of 64 Commander Travis felt it was time to give way to a brilliant successor he himself had personally spotted and groomed. He retired to Pirbright in Surrey with his wife Muriel, and died in 1956.

Joan Clarke

It is difficult to know what this brilliant mathematician would have thought about being portrayed on screen by Keira Knightley. In the 2014 film *The Imitation Game*, Joan Clarke was depicted as a glamorous young woman who made her way to Bletchley almost by chance, having taken part in a cryptic crossword contest. The real Joan Clarke, who died in 1988, might not have objected to the glamour – but to erase the fact that she was actually recruited as a codebreaker because of her fantastic mathematical ability would surely have been felt as an insult. In any event, no film could ever quite do justice to the true enigmas of Joan Clarke's life and career.

Born in 1917 in London and educated at Dulwich High School For Girls, Joan Clarke won a place at Newnham College, Cambridge to study Mathematics, arriving in 1936. Even though women at that time were, extraordinarily, still not awarded the same academic honours as men, she achieved a Double First, winning both a prize and a scholarship for further study.

At the start of the war, it was one of her former tutors who knew that she would be perfect for the formidable challenge of Bletchley Park: Gordon Welchman brought her into the new establishment, where she started on a clerical grade. In order to give her a larger salary, she was promoted to a linguist position, though she had no second language. Before long, she was in Hut 8 – the only woman codebreaker among a team of young men, among whom was Alan Turing. Her manner was apparently perennially gentle and non-confrontational. But her ability shone like a blaze. In the agonised period when the German Navy had added an extra rotor to its Enigma machines, throwing up a seemingly impenetrable barrier to its codes, Joan Clarke was formulating her own methods of cracking them wide open. One was revealed to be the very method devised by Dilly Knox elsewhere: the greatest of minds.

And in the fervid night-shift atmosphere of the time, Clarke and Turing became close. Clarke knew him before Bletchley: her older brother was a friend of Turing. Their relationship developed, as many at Bletchley did, with shared free time picnicking out in the country. Turing asked her to marry him; she said yes. Clarke was careful not to wear the engagement ring on codebreaking shifts: she did not want colleagues and superiors to know.

But Turing then confessed to her that he had 'homosexual tendencies'. Clarke did not want to end the engagement; such matters – almost never discussed anywhere – were not understood then as they are now. But eventually the engagement was broken and the two remained close friends. Clarke later got married in 1952 to another codebreaker, Jock Murray.

The personal story should never overshadow her intellectual achievements: Clarke's cool, quiet manner and capacity for logical and imaginative leaps in the face of insoluble problems made her one of the heroes of the establishment. She received the MBE in 1947; went on to work with the new GCHQ after the war; left in order to move to Scotland with her ailing husband; then returned to GCHQ in 1962, finally retiring in 1977. Her hinterland? An obsessive love for numismatics: the study of historic coins, where she built up a whole new field of expertise.

Alfred Dillwyn Knox

It is sometimes tempting to think that the English archetype of jabbering *Alice in Wonderland* eccentricity is simply a myth. Yet it found perhaps its truest embodiment in a brilliant codebreaker whose career spanned the old and new eras of cryptography.

Dillwyn Knox was, for his young protegés down the years, quite a formidable proposition. Whether sitting in an office bath for hours, staring absently into space, or declaiming *Paradise Lost* with wild gesticulations while driving very fast through the Chiltern Hills, Knox always found new ways to disconcert the uninitiated, even if unintentionally. His name is now revered by today's cryptographers at GCHQ. It was also revered by Churchill who, at a moment of intense crisis for Knox, offered personal help.

Knox, born in 1884, was one of a remarkable clutch of siblings. One brother, Ronald, became a famous Roman Catholic priest and Bible translator; another, Edmund, became a long-running editor of *Punch* magazine. 'Dilly', as Knox was known, had more esoteric expertise, having studied Classics at Cambridge, making friends with John Maynard Keynes and Lytton Strachey along the way.

He was brilliant at deciphering ancient manuscripts, breathing fresh life into long-dead languages, and resurrecting centuries-old accounts of orgies and other unexpectedly pungent subjects. The Great War brought him into Room 40 and, as well as proving a decryption genius, he enlivened the atmosphere with satirical adaptations of Lewis Carroll's Alice stories involving colleagues. It was in Room 40 that he met Olive Rodham, whom he married. And even though after the war he returned to the dusty papyri, his link to codebreaking was now set.

By the 1930s, he was examining the looming challenge of Enigma, and it was he who in 1937 succeeded in cracking the Italian version of the machine by hand. Whether meeting with pioneering Polish mathematicians, or fathoming the workings of a non-functional Enigma machine, or mentoring Alan Turing, or devising a technique known as 'rodding' (like a multi-dimensional slide rule) that helped find a way into the Enigma codes being used in the Spanish Civil War – and thus boosting the general confidence of the codebreakers enormously – Knox had that talent for pure abstraction that enabled him to find tangible solutions to apparently impenetrable mathematical and linguistic problems. This relish for complexity was reflected in his love of Milton's poetry.

New recruits were bamboozled with Carroll-inspired lateral thinking tests (such as 'Which way around do the hands on a clock move?'). The young women he brought into his department were nicknamed 'Dilly's Fillies', though veterans always rightly insisted they were there because Knox thought women had a special affinity with code work.

When the cancer diagnosis came through in 1941, it was understood that, as well as the personal tragedy, Knox's loss would be a terrible blow to the Park. Churchill himself came up with a plan that might help lengthen his days: to have Knox placed on a Naval destroyer and taken to the sunnier climate of the Caribbean, from where he could continue to work. This turned out to be impractical, but Churchill's doctor attended to Knox and ensured he was given incredibly rare access to fresh tropical fruit, which he adored.

When Knox's time came in 1943, his brother Ronald said the final prayers outside his room. Knox turned on his pillow and remarked lightly upon 'Ronnie' being out in the corridor 'bothering God' again.

Nigel de Grey

There were a few codebreakers who might reasonably have been able to claim that they had changed the course of history. Nigel de Grey, a small, modest man who occasionally, and rather dandyishly, wore a cloak, was one such figure. During the Great War in 1917, he (together with Dilly Knox) unravelled a decrypt of seismic importance: a telegram that revealed the Germans were intent on making an alliance with Mexico against the US. Woodrow Wilson's America had been havering about getting embroiled in the European war; this decrypt was hugely influential in tipping the scales decisively for the western Allies. De Grey's feat came to be known as the Zimmerman Telegram.

Born in 1886 and educated at Eton, de Grey began his career by heading into publishing with William Heinemann. The Great War saw him gravitating towards the Balloon Corps and thence into cryptography. At that time it was not a full-time career; the inter-war years brought a period with an upmarket art dealership called the Medici Society (through which de Grey had dealings with Churchill). He loved dramatics, taking to the stage with the Windsor Strollers, and he and his wife Florence would sing, sometimes his own compositions.

With the fight on to defeat Hitler, de Grey was installed in the Park's directorate in the mansion itself, in a first-floor office overlooking the lake and the surrounding huts; at a time of the most furious internal conflicts, de Grey was a steadying influence, and understood very well the need for everyone to find their own pressure valve. As well as art and acting, his also involved shooting and gardening.

As the war ended, he joined a core of colleagues in beginning to build up the successor to Bletchley. He also wrote a (secret) history of the Park's achievements, and the lessons that had to be drawn from it for the future. According to his grandson Michael, de Grey had a 'line of steel' running through him. Michael has also kept the hand-painted birthday cards his extraordinary grandfather sent him when he was a young boy: illustrations replacing words. Nigel de Grey died in 1951, having collapsed with a heart attack on Oxford Street.

Joshua Cooper

While some of the codebreakers might have been accurately described as super-talented amateurs, some of the senior personnel were heavy-duty cryptology professionals. Josh Cooper, the head of Bletchley's Air Section, had years of the most extraordinary experience behind him. In 1930 he was in Sarafand, unravelling Soviet coded messages across the Black Sea; he was penetrating Italian encryptions in the early 1930s, focusing on that nation's air force at a time when the lethal science of bombing was being formulated.

And yet, like so many of his colleagues at the Park, Cooper somehow managed to acquire rather more fame for his quirky mannerisms. Never mind that he was fluent in Arabic as well as Russian; what was gossiped about was the moment when he was striding around the lake and – talking to himself – hurled his mug of tea into it to underline the point he had been making to himself. Then there was the time he was conducting an interrogation of a German officer shot down from the sky; in a moment of confusion, Cooper – a large man – contrived to fall off his chair, to the bewilderment of the cowed prisoner.

The stories essentially spoke of affection: Cooper was large of stature and nicknamed 'the Bear', but he had a gentle nature. Born in 1901, he had (a small world, this) been briefly taught by Dilly Knox's elder priest brother Ronald at Shrewsbury. Cooper attended the University of London, where his skill with languages – he almost unthinkingly acquired every European tongue – flourished. By 1925, he had been recruited for the Government Code and Cypher School, and now cryptography would occupy the rest of his working life.

In 1944 he was promoted to Deputy Director of Bletchley Park. One of his great achievements at the Park was ensuring that the outstations – known as the Y- (or 'Wireless') Service – were used properly. These outposts, from Cheadle to Cairo, were also filled with hugely talented young people.

After the war, Cooper remained in the shadows with the Cold War codebreakers, a key figure in the newly formed GCHQ. The enemy now was Russia, yet Cooper had lost none of his love and fascination for the Russian language and the riches of Russian literature. He went on to publish several books on the subject, before his death in 1961.

Arthur Bonsall

A sense of duty about secrecy and discretion governed Arthur Bonsall's life long after Bletchley Park; even at a veterans' reunion day at the site a few years ago, he maintained a Sphinx-like silence when accosted by puppyish reporters about his career. This was certainly not haughtiness. Bonsall had risen, years after the war, to become Director of GCHQ. Up until the 1980s, even those initials were kept out of the public domain. It was a department that was never officially acknowledged: the risk of leaks to hostile powers was simply too great. But Arthur Bonsall in his own way encapsulated the ethos of Bletchley Park (and decades later was instrumental in the site being saved).

Born in Middlesbrough in 1917, Bonsall read French, German and Russian at Cambridge; it was there that he was talent-spotted (together with Harry Hinsley), and he arrived to work at Hut 4 under Josh Cooper. There was no preliminary training; he was simply directed to a trestle table with a pile of coded communications. Bletchley was not all about Enigma: there was also the business of traffic analysis, and exploration of huge quantities of low-level coded material that added small elements to an ever more detailed mosaic of intelligence, giving three-dimensional background to a raft of other messages. By 1944, the gifted Bonsall was transferred to an even more secret department within a department: a collaboration between Bletchley and MI6 focusing on Soviet codes. The base for this was a house in Chelsea just off Sloane Square.

Lifelong Codebreakers

Such a life was clearly impossible to consider leaving. And as GCHQ moved to Cheltenham, so Bonsall took charge of a division monitoring and analysing the coded traffic from eastern Europe at a time of convulsions in east Berlin, and Hungary. Bonsall gradually moved from this to develop fresh expertise in intelligence from the equally fraught Middle East, as Israel's neighbours sought to destroy the new nation. And it was in 1973, as he rose to become director of GCHQ, that Bonsall flew personally to Washington DC to draw on all his powers of discretion and help re-establish the incredibly close Special Relationship in codebreaking that had been fractured by Prime Minister Edward Heath's reluctance to follow President Nixon's every foreign policy move. The repairs were successfully made.

After a career of uncommon intensity, Sir Arthur Bonsall retired in 1978; though now, with the veil just starting to lift, it was possible for him to begin a new pursuit of carefully curating aspects of the Park's history, ensuring that its less glamorous successes – compiling a vast source of data from carefully analysed global communications traffic – were put on the map. On that Veterans' Reunion Day, as he gazed around the beautifully restored house and the grounds, it was clear he was suffused with pride. He died in Cheltenham in 2014.

Margaret Rock

Much of her working life was spent in the shadows; but in that twilight, her secret achievements glowed all the more brightly. Margaret Rock is now celebrated by GCHQ, for which she worked with distinction. Together with Joan Clarke (still best known, unfairly, as Alan Turing's fiancée), she was among the few pioneering women who helped shape the organisation that now monitors a universe of cyber-communications. Yet she is not a household name, and cannot be for some years to come yet, for the bulk of her sensitive intelligence work is still covered by the Official Secrets Act. Happily, her Bletchley legacy is celebrated.

Although it might not have been a perfect meritocracy, Bletchley Park was nonetheless fantastically nimble when it came to recognising talent. Margaret Rock, recruited in April 1940 as a 'Junior Administrative Assistant', had a flair for mathematics and, with her posting to 'the Cottage', alongside Mavis Lever and working for Dilly Knox, that aptitude at last found a chance for expression. Knox — renowned for absent-mindedly attempting to fill his pipe with a half-eaten sandwich as opposed to tobacco — was so excited by Margaret Rock's skill that after a few weeks he wrote a memo: 'Miss Rock is entirely in the wrong grade. She is actually 4th or 5th best of all the Enigma staff and quite as useful as some of the "professors". I recommend that she be put on the highest possible salary for someone of her seniority.'

But even before Bletchley, Margaret Rock's analytic skills had been admired. Born in west London in 1903 and educated in north-east

Lifelong Codebreakers

London (the rough-and-ready industrial district of Edmonton), she went on to the University of London and was then employed through the 1920s by the National Association of Manufacturers: her role was that of a statistician. This might sound dry, but, amid the economic earthquakes of that decade, she was analysing international markets and attempting to find safe waters for businesses being flung about on those tempestuous waves. She also had a passion for foreign travel at a time when it was far from common, and an easy familiarity with life in Europe.

This broad outlook, combined with the ability to bring order to the apparent chaos, of either market reports or encryptions, in many senses made her the ideal recruit for Bletchley, and her work with Mavis Lever, Keith Batey and Peter Twinn on prising open the Abwehr codes – an invaluable trove of intelligence at the war's most intense moments in 1944 – was both historic and also far too secret to be aired in public until many decades had passed.

After the war, she was made an MBE (codebreakers who were honoured naturally had the reasons for those citations censored) and, along with Joan Clarke, she was persuaded by the authorities to continue codebreaking. As Europe froze into the Cold War, Margaret Rock became one of the mainstays of the post-Bletchley department that would soon regenerate into GCHQ, and she stayed with GCHQ until her retirement aged 60 in 1983.

Sadly, she died later that year. Pleasingly, her contribution to wartime codebreaking – including a formerly banned account of the joint effort to crack the Abwehr – has now officially made it into the history books; GCHQ itself proudly salutes one of its great pioneers.

Brigadier John Tiltman

Not all coded puzzles came from the enemy; sometimes there were more ancient enigmas from the past to be tackled. One such was known as 'the Voynich Manuscript' — a mysterious, quasi-occultist document containing weird miniature paintings involving alchemy, naked ladies and a wholly unknown language. It was rumoured to have dated from the sixteenth-century court of Emperor Rudolf in Prague. The manuscript had turned up in a New York book dealers at the start of the twentieth century, and by the Second World War had been passed to US codebreakers. What could these unintelligible letters and images mean? How could one interpret the diagrams of naked homunculi in glass jars with impenetrable inscriptions beneath? American cryptographers knew instantly whom they wished to consult: Bletchley Park's Brigadier John Tiltman.

Even now, the US National Security Agency hails Tiltman, known as 'the Brig', as one of the greatest of all cryptanalysts. His achievements at the Park were prodigious. Not only did he teach himself a way into the most abstruse of Japanese encryptions; he also set up a special codebreakers school in Bedford which imparted his knowledge, plus a lightning course in the Japanese language, to the brightest of the new codebreakers. Tiltman — who always wore his own version of uniform, including tartan trews, but barked at younger recruits who tried to emulate his military example, telling them to get rid of those damn boots — was one of the Park's greatest forgotten geniuses.

Lifelong Codebreakers

His was a precocious intellect. Born in 1894, Tiltman was offered a place at Cambridge at the age of 13. His father's premature death meant the family finances would not stretch to it. The First World War brought the young man into the King's Own Scottish Borderers; he was injured in 1917 and was awarded the Military Cross. In 1919, his career in espionage began, as he was sent with a few others on a mission to Siberia, partly to support the counter-revolutionaries.

Tiltman never claimed to be a linguist, but the Russian he acquired subsequently made him sought after for other postings (including analysing Soviet traffic in Asia), and eventually a position at the Government Code and Cypher School, heading a military section with an increasing number of communications – Russian, German, Italian, Japanese – to deal with.

The Brig was not in any formal sense a mathematician either, but he had an instinct for systems and structure that enabled him to burrow into different styles of encryption with the power of abstract thought. At Bletchley Park the full range of his experience – different encryption techniques, and by now a huge variety of languages – was brought to bear on everything from the Japanese Purple codes to the Nazis' Abwehr system. It was Tiltman, working in the mansion's old nursery, in a room decorated with Peter Rabbit wallpaper, who began to uncover, through decrypts, the horror of the Holocaust.

The life of codebreaking was not easily forsaken, and after the war Tiltman could not let this genius go to waste. His American counterparts were so enamoured of him that he was invited over to the US, first as a special liaison officer operating out of the British Embassy in Washington, and then as a fresh new recruit (at the age of around 60) into the National Security Agency. This was an honour given to very few, an ultimate gesture of trust and love.

Incredibly, he worked on in Washington DC until 1980. Then at the age of 85, he retired to Hawaii, and died two years later. Alas, one of the few codes to have eluded him was that of the Voynich Manuscript, which remains fathomlessly mysterious and unknowable – or indeed, a wry and complex sixteenth-century satirical hoax.

THE JEWISH EXPERIENCE

Walter Eytan

In some corners of Britain's security services throughout the 1930s and in the post-war years, there were pockets of fierce anti-Semitism. This rarely seemed to be a serious issue at Bletchley Park: many of its finest recruits and minds were Jewish. But after the war, as Zionism reached its zenith in the wake of the Holocaust, there were outbreaks of – at best – ambivalence once again in the intelligence community.

Walter Eytan and his brother were particularly conscious of this. But nothing was going to stop Walter Eytan joining the State of Israel on its foundation in 1948. He was to become one of the country's most notable figures. Perhaps some of the intellectual dexterity that he developed at Bletchley was of assistance as he made a career establishing diplomatic relations with other nations across the world.

He was born Maurice Ettinghausen in Munich, 1910, but his parents came to London, where he was educated. He studied at Queen's College, Oxford, specialising in Latin, Greek, and German philology, and he stayed there as a tutor, teaching German literature. Such a mind, combined with such a fine knowledge of the German language, was too valuable to be overlooked, and in 1940 he was one of the earliest recruits to Bletchley Park. He was initially bemused that someone born in Germany could pass the security vetting, but also reasoned to himself that the Bletchley authorities, knowing he was Jewish, had calculated that his determination to defeat Hitler would be all the stronger.

The Jewish Experience

By the end of the war, he understood with the utmost clarity that nowhere in Europe could be counted safe for Jewish people; a homeland was the most urgent moral necessity. In 1946, he travelled for what was still then British Mandate Palestine and joined the government-in-waiting. After the war of 1948 Eytan, as Foreign Minister, was a key figure in establishing diplomatic recognition for Israel from nations that might have been reluctant. He had fantastic energy; after a frenetic diplomatic career, some years spent as ambassador to Paris, he headed up the Israeli Broadcasting Authority.

It was at Bletchley that he had received the first inkling of the horror that the Nazis were perpetrating in the dark forests of the east. 'In late 1943 or early 1944', he wrote, 'we intercepted a signal from a small . . . vessel in the Aegean, reporting that it was transporting Jews . . . *zur Endlosung* ['for the Final Solution']. I had never seen or heard this expression before but instinctively I knew what it must mean, and I have never forgotten that moment.'

Rolf Noskwith

Ladies in post-war north London associated the name of Charnos with fine-quality stockings and lingerie. In the austere 1950s, not long after rationing had finally ended, such items could carry a sense of luxury. As a trade, it was sometimes the butt of saucy end-of-pier comedians, but there was a very dignified and rather moving reality behind this particular business. It was a family concern, founded so that that family might find a measure of security in a darkening world.

In its post-war years, however, the man who ran it had already faced quite a different prospective path: that of lending his formidable intellect to the government of the newly established state of Israel.

Rolf Noskwith had already proved to be one of Britain's most adept cryptographers. Yet if elements of the security services in the early 1940s had had their way, he would not even have been allowed as far as the Bletchley Park canteen. The difficulty was that he had been born in Germany. His parents were Polish Jews – the family name was Noskovitch – who owned a clothing business in Chemnitz, in the east of the country. They emigrated in 1932, a little before Hitler came to power, partly on account of the menacing horizon, but also to escape punitive tariffs: it would be more viable to set up in England's Midlands.

Young Noskwith (who went to school in Nottingham) was an intensely clever undergraduate at Trinity College, Cambridge, and in 1941 the codebreakers decided they must have him. The security vetters at MI5 were having none of it. But the codebreakers pushed harder: Noskwith was interviewed by both Hugh Alexander and the novelist C. P. Snow, who had a liaison role. And so the 22-year-old was inducted into Hut 8 at the height of the Battle of the Atlantic. On top of the intensity of his duties, Noskwith was there to witness the emotional intensity of Alan Turing's engagement to Joan Clarke.

In the fight against the naval ciphers – failure would have meant ever more convoys being sunk by ever more U-boats, threatening food supplies – there was no let-up, and Noskwith was to recall how the insane pressure, combined with the fearsome complexity of the task, became addictive. When the war ended, he could not face returning to ordinary life straight away, and so transferred to the post-war codebreaking operation at Eastcote, on the fringes of west London.

He also stood at an historical crossroads. In 1946, fellow codebreaker Walter Eytan, by then a senior figure in the struggle to establish Israel as a Jewish state, asked Noskwith to join him. When the state was at last founded in 1948 his pulsing intelligence would have been a terrific asset.

Noskwith had another destiny to fulfil, however: taking over the family business. There was a substantial distance between the exhilaration of Hut 8 and the selling of lingerie, but he was keeping the family heritage alive. In 1957 he married Annette Greenbaum, who had come to England on the *Kindertransport*. At Bletchley, he had thrown himself not merely into winning a war, but also into ensuring a future where he and his family could feel secure. Those who have not known persecution take safety for granted. Noskwith was poignantly aware just how easily it could be ripped away. His contribution to the defeat of the Nazis had an particularly practical dimension.

Sidney Goldberg

It must have been quite an extraordinary moment for Sidney Goldberg in 2009 when he received the award from then Foreign Secretary David Milliband. Over 60 years since his secret work in the Middle East sent invaluable intelligence back to the codebreakers, he was now finally there in Bletchley Park to be honoured for it.

But then it was a life punctuated with the extraordinary. Sidney Goldberg had been born in Leipzig, Germany, in 1923. The lengthening shadow over the country darkening further, in 1933 an uncle managed to arrange for the boy to come to London, where he started afresh at the Jewish Free School. Thankfully, a little later, his parents made it out of Germany too. The Nazis had started charging Jewish people ransoms to leave; by this means they stole huge amounts of property. Other members of Goldberg's family did not make it, and in the years that followed were deported to the forests of the east and the death camps.

The young Goldberg was eager to do whatever he could for his new country. The RAF was his desire – a fellow young German Jew, Ken Adam, took this route and became a brilliant fighter pilot; later he became better known as the production designer for the Bond films – but Goldberg's eyesight was a problem.

What he did have, of course, was brilliantly fluent German. As war came, he was drafted into 381 Wireless Unit, and he and his team were sent to North Africa, moving from Algeria to Tunisia, all the time intercepting and tracking Luftwaffe signals and messages.

The Jewish Experience

This unit was an integral part of the Y-Service, the fruits of whose endeavours made their way back to the Air Ministry, and on to Bletchley Park for analysis and cross reference. Even as the war turned decisively in favour of the Allies, and Goldberg and his unit went to Sicily, theirs was a role with its own distinct hazards: capture would have meant nightmare interrogation and for Goldberg, of German Jewish heritage, even more terrible possibilities, both as a perceived 'traitor' and as potential forced labour material.

The years after the war brought rather quieter dealings in the textile trade, with Goldberg becoming involved with the Prince's Trust charity. He was also passionate about the welfare and memories of other veterans, and was instrumental in ensuring that the fiftieth anniversary of the D-Day landings in 1994 was commemorated with the utmost panache and dignity. Along the way he was also awarded the prestigious French decoration of Chevalier de la Légion d'honneur. Without the brave work of Goldberg, among many thousands of other Y-Service recruits, Bletchley would have been running on empty.

Ruth Sebag Montefiore

The freewheeling atmosphere of the Park made it perfect not only for eccentric codebreakers, but also for astute and witty social observers. Ruth Sebag Montefiore was 23 years old and engaged in secretarial work for the Foreign Office when war broke out; very soon, she was invited to Broadway Buildings near St James's Park for an interview about being sent to a new establishment in Buckinghamshire. It was a very connected world: Bletchley Park's original owner Sir Herbert Leon had in fact been her great uncle.

So by the time she arrived, the house already had an echo of familiarity, even if its new incarnation had brought many changes. 'Only by stretching my imagination to the utmost,' she wrote, 'could I picture the place . . . in its heyday, when there were hunters in the stables, house parties most weekends and children in the top-floor nurseries.'

What was also unfamiliar, in those first few weeks and months of Bletchley, was the spectacle of quite so many people of extraordinary habits clustered together, either in rooms in the main house, or in the huts beyond which were 'beginning to sprout up like mushrooms'. 'Brilliant minds', she wrote years later of her codebreaking colleagues, 'interesting individually, but collectively, when they poured out of the huts for breaks, they looked like beings from another planet.'

Before the fiery sparks of mathematical genius turned Bletchley into a world-dominating cipher factory, there was sometimes a more

The Jewish Experience

valiantly amateur approach. In her own department, Ruth Sebag Montefiore found herself dealing with coded telegrams to and from agents in the field. These involved everything from U-boat sightings to concealing escaped POWs. She was privy to an extraordinary range of material; on one occasion, as she recalled, she saw a coded telegram from the head of MI6 Sir Stewart Menzies asking after the health of her cousin Tim Cohen, who had been seriously injured in north Africa. Sir Stewart, it seemed, was a good friend of Cohen's father. Ruth Sebag Montefiore ensured that the communication got top priority.

For a time, she was in Hut 10, which was 'run by a retired general, ill at ease with sixty women.' But there was also a department head called Miss Montgomery from the Foreign Office, who resembled Miss Marple in both dress sense and in having a steel-trap mind. There were curious anomalies thrown up by Bletchley life: because it was so intensely secret, Ruth Sebag Montefiore recalled, she did not pay income tax. 'This annoyed my bank manager when I was unable to tell him what I did!'

The later years of the war brought new and different adventures: a codebreaking posting at the end of 1944 to Eindhoven, for which she was required to wear ATS uniform in case she was ever suspected of working for intelligence and thus becoming a potential target for agents of the enemy. Her future brought a more tranquil career of books and memoirs. She wrote the evocative *A Family Patchwork: Five Generations of an Anglo-Jewish Family*, and became something of a literary matriarch herself. And her association with Bletchley also helped shine a further light of historical interest on the Establishment's especially strong relationship with the Jewish community.

TEACHERS

Mr Denniston

A preparatory school in the 1950s in the small Surrey dormitory town of Leatherhead. It is easy to imagine the quietly spoken schoolmaster who teaches French and Latin with drawn face, slightly stooped, as might befall one who had in his youth been an Olympic athlete. He is very good at imparting knowledge, but the boys listening to their greying teacher do not – cannot – know anything of their teacher's previous life. There is yet more poignancy in knowing that their own lives, filled with war comics and adventure novels, would have been brightened wildly to learn that this man had been a master cryptographer – in fact, nothing less than the leader of the codebreakers, and instrumental in shortening the war and saving illimitable lives. It is a haunting image somehow redolent of a John le Carré story.

Recognition came too late for Alastair Denniston, the naval commander who set up the entire Bletchley Park operation. Indeed, he was also, in the truest sense, the first head of what we would now call GCHQ, and the operatives at GCHQ now take pains to honour him in their official histories. But the career of Alastair Guthrie Denniston was marked with rough reversals, and there were many who thought he was treated shabbily by his Foreign Office superiors. There was one consolation: his life contained many more strands than codebreaking.

Alastair Denniston, born at the height of the Victorian age in 1881 to Scottish parents, was an adventurous student who studied

Teachers

languages at the universities of Paris and Bonn. Teaching seemed an obvious career, but he sidestepped slightly into giving German and French language tutorials to senior naval personnel.

The sidestep grew more pronounced at the outbreak of the Great War, when he was drawn into becoming one of the founding cryptologists in a Whitehall department called Room 40. (It was in this department that he met his wife to be, Dorothy Gilliat – they were pioneers when it came to illuminating the unexpected codebreaking side-effect of romance.) After that war, Denniston had argued that codebreaking remained vital, and so it was under his aegis that the Government Code and Cypher School came into being.

As a younger man, in 1908, Denniston had competed at the Olympics, in the Scottish hockey team. The sport's tough physicality might have been some preparation for the intense and bloody internal politics of the intelligence services. As a naval commander in the 1930s, Denniston was alive to the multiple hazards Britain faced should war break out again. And he – together with Dilly Knox – was swift about catching up on Enigma and how it might be defeated, using the expertise of the three brilliant Polish mathematicians who had first found a way into the machine.

It was therefore under Denniston that a generation of unruly geniuses was gathered at Bletchley. Even now, in the archives, it is possible to read his memos on all subjects from sensitive staffing issues to the disgrace of missing canteen crockery. Yet while he got the operation running, Denniston was perhaps slow to realise the extraordinary extent of its potential. By 1942, he had been shunted sideways to a London department working on diplomatic traffic – a very successful department, but a demotion none the less – and it was his deputy Edward Travis who transformed Bletchley into a vast codebreaking factory.

Given the intense secrecy, the end of the war then brought obscurity (although Denniston had received the due honour of the CBE and CMG). Aged 64, and not in especially good health, he returned to his original career: teaching. He lived until 1961; long enough at least to see the intelligence organisation he had founded move to Cheltenham and become ever more renowned throughout the (highly classified) world. It was left to his son, Robin, who became a notable publisher, to publish a biography of his father over forty years later.

Mr Balme

Is knowledge of the Classics necessary or relevant? The current Prime Minister, who rarely lets any occasion to parade his own expertise in this field pass by, would argue yes. But even back in the 1960s, when Latin was still commonly taught in comprehensive and public schools alike, the subject looked to be fading. Maurice Balme was one of a team of Classics masters who had the idea of re-inventing the subject by dropping the rote declensions and introducing lively narrative texts for beginners. The exploits of Caecelius and his family are still fondly remembered by the 1970s generation (including this author). It was that sort of lateral approach that had led Balme to being recruited for Bletchley's Japanese codebreaking operation.

Born in 1925, Balme had begun his wartime career with the Royal Marines. But there was a curious and coincidental family connection to Bletchley that had been forged some time before he got there. His brother David Balme had led the extraordinary 1941 boarding party which clambered aboard the stricken German submarine U110 in the Mediterranean, managing to haul from it an invaluable Enigma machine and (if possible, even more invaluable) its accompanying codebook. This was the material that brought the greatest leap forward in the Battle of the Atlantic, and in other theatres. The sub-lieutenant would not have been at liberty to tell his younger brother precisely what it was that he had achieved. But Maurice Balme arrived at a Bletchley Park that was a world-beating code-cracking factory, and was one of the adepts sent to a secret tutorial room above a gas showroom in nearby Bedford for his crash course in Japanese, and Japanese encryptions.

And so rather than having been recruited because of his expertise in Classics, Balme acquired that knowledge after the war. His first move was to study at Trinity College, Oxford. He then became a master at Harrow School, staying there for many years and becoming Head of Classics. As well as finding innovative ways to reinvigorate the field for the younger generation, he also worked on popular translations for Oxford World's Classics. And he left a lasting legacy: a beginner's Greek course called *Athenaze*, featuring a vivid adventurous fifth-century BC narrative, a relatable hero and exquisite grammar, all of which was published by the Oxford University Press and remains the most popular of such courses. Bletchley's greatest classicist Dilly Knox would have declaimed with approval.

Mr Townend

As we have seen with Commander Alastair Denniston, the image of former intelligence men who end up teaching at public schools is curiously melancholic. Yet there is no reason why this should have been the case in real life; teaching is a grand vocation and there were those among the codebreakers of Bletchley who took to it strongly following the war. Another such was Brian Townend: he was a master at the famous Dragon School in Oxford, and he taught classics and music at Sevenoaks School. None of his pupils will have had a notion of what he did during the war. Yet they will have sensed the sharp intellect (and indeed easy facility with languages) that would have suggested something other than a role in fatigues.

Indeed, Townend's codebreaking war took him from Bletchley to Kenya, where there was an decryption outstation at Kilindini, not far from Mount Kilimanjaro, which some fellow codebreakers could not resist attempting. It was at this base that Japanese naval codes were attacked, and from which invaluable technical terms were gleaned and cross-referenced. It was a tight-knit team that scored some notable successes against some of the most apparently intransigent ciphers.

From there Townend later sailed further east to HMS Anderson in Colombo, where he met his wife-to-be Bett, a Wren who had been posted there to work on some of the fearsome machinery. HMS Anderson was in some ways very military – there were inspections and parades for the Wrens – but had a distinctly exotic nightlife, involving plush Colombo clubs and hotel ballrooms. Townend, born in 1917, had read Greats at Oxford, and it was for his linguistic flair that he was originally approached. He went through the fast Japanese course at Bedford, and he also acquired Russian along the way.

Many who had tasted life in Colombo could not face the psychic shock of cold, grim, post-war Britain – Jean Valentine and her husband escaped back east as soon as they could. But Brian Townend was fixed upon teaching. If only he could ever have told his pupils of his wartime achievements . . .

Mr Roseveare

The esteemed political commentator Matthew Parris has warm memories of his childhood mathematics teacher: a man, he wrote, 'of gentle merriment', an explosive giggle and an enthusiasm for the operas of Gilbert and Sullivan. Young master Parris would have had no inkling decades ago of his teacher's extraordinary hinterland.

In some ways, it was rather moving that Robert Roseveare should choose to focus his post-war life on teaching; it was something of a family tradition. But in another way, the secrecy was a shame: imagine if he had been able to teach mathematics by using codebreaking problems – even the most reluctant and innumerate pupils would have been saucer-eyed and avid to know more.

Moreover, Roseveare, born in 1923, was a remarkable recruit to Bletchley Park because he was one of the few who were drawn directly from school: he had been in the sixth form at Marlborough when he was selected to work in Hut 6 alongside Gordon Welchman's team. This had happened just after he had been offered a scholarship to read mathematics at St John's College, Oxford.

The carefree days of university would have to wait until after the war. Before then came the careworn business of burrowing daily into the ever-changing encryptions of the Luftwaffe. As well as his mathematical prowess, Roseveare also had the analytic ability to work on the weightier longer-term decryptions as opposed to the instantaneous messages of everyday traffic. Nor did he step down immediately after victory was won in Europe: he transferred to the

Japanese section until August 1945. It was at Bletchley that he met the woman who would become his wife.

After university, there was a brief foray into retail management at John Lewis. But Roseveare was also, like Bletchley's pioneer director Alastair Denniston, a rather gifted hockey player, and it was when an international competition took him to South Africa that he fell in love with that wide landscape. He and his family moved to Natal, then Johannesburg, as he taught mathematics; given the nature of South African society then, it must also be noted that he helped set up a multi-racial school in Swaziland, where he was made a lay preacher.

But by 1965 he was back in England; by 1970, he was teaching at Uppingham, and was head of mathematics until 1983. The art of untangling problems, and presenting solutions: the thread connecting the back-room blackboards of Bletchley to the many classrooms that followed.

POLITICS AND
THE DIPLOMATIC WORLD

Lord Jenkins of Hillhead

ONE of the less celebrated skills in life is knowing, and admitting, that you are not particularly good at something. Given that Roy Jenkins was to achieve such a colossal amount after the war – Home Secretary, Chancellor of the Exchequer, President of the European Commission, the man who remade the entire landscape of 1980s British politics, plus on top of all this a bestselling historian and biographer – it does him great credit that he admitted that his time spent cracking codes at Bletchley Park was not a stellar success.

Yet that modesty may have been misplaced. Jenkins had been a captain with the Royal Artillery when he had been pulled into Bletchley Park in 1942. He was part of Ralph Tester's team, in the department known as 'the Testery', and stayed there until the end of the war. He and his colleagues were focusing on the Lorenz machine telecipher system, which was being used by senior Nazi personnel throughout Europe. The work clearly had its frustrations, but there were results. For a time, Jenkins found himself working alongside John Herivel, the young mathematician whose 1940 hunch had really set the entire codebreaking operation into action on an industrial scale. These days, in GCHQ's own archives, we can see that Jenkins was also reprimanded for 'misappropriating Bletchley Park lunch sandwich tickets': morally on a par with the debs who adopted disguises to re-join the lunch queue for extra helpings.

Among all the more senior intellects, Jenkins was in any case something of a prodigy. The son of a Welsh collier turned politician, he was born in Pontypool in 1920. By 1938, he was walking through the gates of Balliol College, Oxford. Despite the war, he managed to continue his studies until being called up. And after the war, and the necessary constraints of Bletchley, he wasted no time in beginning to build his political career within the Labour Party.

He was arguably one of the most influential politicians of the age. His time within Harold Wilson's government was notable for his backing the legalisation of homosexuality, and instituting proper race relations policies. He was a passionate pro-European, partly as a result of the war, and the conviction that it should never happen again. His fondness for fine wines was mocked fondly.

Though his codebreaking days remained under wraps for decades, there were still chance meetings at cocktail parties with old faces: when the Hon. Sarah Baring bumped into him one evening in the 1970s there were no words: just a big, broad wink from Jenkins.

Nancy Joan Seligman

The former prime minister Edward Heath, who governed from 1970 to 1974, was renowned for his lack of charm and social awkwardness. Yet Nancy Joan Seligman was one of the handful of people who could coax him into something approaching friendly warmth. This was a singular skill that must have been studied closely by the politicians and civil servants obliged to work alongside the Tory leader.

But her vivacity had been noted in many other quarters. Born in 1918 in south London – Nancy's mother was American and her father was instrumental in setting up the *Financial Times* – she swiftly became attuned to the delights and absurdities of high-society conventions. In the 1930s, Nancy was a debutante, but suffered a calamity when the trail of her dress dropped into a lavatory. She was also partly educated in France, which gave her a linguistic facility. Added to all this, her godfather was Rudyard Kipling. All these social connections, plus the personal energy, must have made her one of the more obvious choices for Bletchley Park.

Yet it seems her role there was more active than many others. She was a very keen driver, and happy to fulfil that role for the Park's directorate. At other points in the war, she drove ambulances. Nancy Joan Seligman embodied that *Tatler* 'It Girl' persona of thoroughly trustworthy recruit that was favoured in the early days.

After the war her cosmopolitan personality found further expression when at last she married her long-term love, Madron Seligman, an industrialist and passionate European. He won a seat at the very first European Parliament, established in 1979, and held it for fifteen years, which meant Nancy became a mainstay in the Brussels political and diplomatic scene.

That commitment to Europe was very much there in the Seligmans' friendship with Edward Heath, who in 1973 had taken the UK into the EEC. Throughout his premiership Nancy and Madron (Madron and Heath had been at Oxford together) spent their Christmases at Chequers, where she brought the spirit of the season to a wintry, lonely and largely unloved Prime Minister.

Edgar Harrison

Bletchley Park was at the centre of a web, the threads of which extended across the world. In the face of the hostile invasion of distant territories, from Greece to the Far East, such a network could seem frighteningly fragile. Yet the Y-Service and the department of MI6 known as Section VIII kept the threads taut and strong. And heading up the Special Communications Unit was a courageous and proactive soldier who had signed up for signals work back in 1929 aged just 14.

Edgar Harrison was an Ultra intelligence officer who, when not training agents at Bletchley, or sticking by Churchill's side as the Prime Minister made international forays, threw himself into the heart of the action, from Crete to Yugoslavia. He was the means by which the decryptions from Bletchley were disseminated, with maximum security, to the military hierarchy, and by which communications links were kept open when all around apparent anarchy reigned in a storm of bullets and mortars.

His zeal for signals work, possibly prompted by a passion for radio technology, very common among teenage boys in the 1920s and 1930s, had originally led him to sign up for an apprenticeship with the Royal Corps of Signals. The schoolboy was packed off to Catterick in Yorkshire for training. His skill with Morse and codes then led to 1930s postings to China (involving some covert signals work) and Hong Kong.

At the start of the war, he received the typically enigmatic invite to Bletchley – a railway ticket and a letter not to be opened until he was aboard the train – and this in turn led to Harrison teaching super-speedy Morse to agents then sent out into the field.

When he went out into the wartime field himself, first to Athens, life was eventful. In 1941 he took part in a bayonet charge on Crete; then he spent time in the North African desert; then he was parachuted into Yugoslavia to help foment the anti-Nazi forces. In addition to all of this, he was frequently by Churchill's side while flying to conferences so that he could keep the PM briefed on all the latest Ultra intelligence, enabling him to stay ahead of the diplomatic game.

This life was not easily given up for a quiet retirement, and so Harrison, awarded a Military Cross and a British Empire Medal and made Captain, continued after the war with the Diplomatic Wireless Service, his expertise in covert signals taking him to serve in Tokyo and Moscow. He was in charge of communications (straightforward and top secret) from the embassies; the once schoolboy enthusiast now monitoring the most sensitive currents of the Cold War. He was awarded the OBE for services to the Foreign and Commonwealth Office.

Patricia Brown

One of the curious curses of life after Bletchley Park was the struggle to find new occupations that would spark that obsessive intensity. To be the wife of a diplomat – although not in any way an unworthy position – was never going to match that electrical charge of achievement.

Patricia Bartley, married to a fellow Oxford graduate called Denys Brown who was posted throughout the 1950s, 1960s and 1970s throughout Europe and instrumental in preparing the UK's entry into the EEC, was 'cut off' from 'any intellectually fulfilling role'. None the less, she attempted to stretch herself in different ways. She became fluent in five languages. No-one she ever spoke to at any of the ambassador's receptions was allowed to know that she was one of the most highly regarded female codebreakers at Bletchley.

A child of empire, born in Dhaka where her father, a judge, was a senior civil servant, Patricia Bartley was among the first to be summoned to the Buckinghamshire mansion, recruited partly for her expertise with the German language and partly, it is thought, because she had come to the attention of a family friend and veteran codebreaker, Emily Anderson. Armed only with a pencil and scarcely any induction, Patricia was set to work on a German code known at Bletchley as 'Floradora'. Even though the hours were brutal and the food was 'dreadful', there was also pride: a success in finding some 'regularities' in the ciphers which brought fresh possibilities of prying them open.

Transferred to the cipher operation in Berkeley Street in Mayfair (where Alastair Denniston had been sent to head up the Diplomatic decoding section), Patricia Bartley was also among those who had intensive dealings with American codebreakers, some of whom, with cheerful sexism, declared themselves smitten with her 'brains, beauty and vivacity'; a step up from the scenario of a woman scientist being told that she looks captivating without her glasses. The general strain, though, was unendurable, and by 1943, Patricia Bartley was forced to bow out. She moved into the Foreign Office, where she later became adept with anti-Soviet material.

In later years, when the secrecy dropped, she was briskly unsentimental about her time at Bletchley, though she noted wryly that perhaps the most discreet people of all might have been the townsfolk themselves. After all, she said, 'they must had had a pretty good idea of what was going on.'

Margaret Cooper

For some, the intensity of the war gave way afterwards to lives of determined tranquility. This was the case for a woman who had been at the heart of Bletchley, who eventually devoted herself to farming and politics in Canada – being particularly sought out for a hug by Justin Trudeau during his 2015 election campaign. But Margaret Cooper's life had never run along predictable rails, and her time at the Park also produced one of its sweetest romantic vignettes.

She was born Margaret Douglas in 1918 on a beef ranch in Argentina (her family was well-to-do Anglo-Argentine). Sent to board at St Mary's School in Wantage, Dorset, she subsequently returned to Buenos Aires and moved into a 1930s moneyed life of tennis and polo. The shadow of war, however, inspired her in a different direction, and she returned to Britain to volunteer for the Wrens. There was a possibility, early on, that she might have been a cook (perhaps around the time when Alastair Denniston was insisting in memos that the authorities should not send him 'too many of the Cook and Messenger types'). An aptitude test changed everything; that, plus a mysterious indication from her superiors that she and others were needed for a project of the most intense secrecy . . .

Thus it was that she arrived at Bletchley, working first in Hut 11 on the Bombe machines, which were at that point focused on decrypts from the Desert War. A stint at Bletchley's outstation in Stanmore in north-west London followed: a new department of Bombe machines had been set up there. After all this came a return to Bletchley and promotion to be the ebullient Frank Birch's executive assistant in Hut 4, working against U-boat codes. She also liaised with the Admiralty in Whitehall.

It was one misty night on the platform of Bletchley railway station in 1942 that she struck up a conversation with a Canadian Air Force officer waiting for the London train. He was instantly smitten, but his train departed before he had even managed to catch the young woman's name.

What followed was a bold move. He wrote a letter addressed to 'The Blonde Wren From Argentina On The Platform At Bletchley Station'. Incredibly, the letter eventually reached her. After the war, they married, and moved to Canada. A long life of farming and teaching followed. It was only decades later that she could tell her railway platform beau precisely what it was she had been doing there in the first place.

MAVERICKS, RENEGADES AND 'QUIET LIVES'

Baroness Trumpington
(Jean Campbell Harris)

There are some Establishment figures who are, paradoxically, anti-Establishment. The image of Baroness Trumpington in the House of Lords flicking a V-sign at another peer is a perfect example. It earned her an invitation to appear on the satirical BBC panel show *Have I Got News For You*; newspapers clamoured to print her salty opinions.

That said, it is possible no-one was ever quite brave enough to ask the formidable baroness if it was true she had once been loaded into a laundry basket on wheels at Bletchley Park, pushed down the corridor at tremendous speed, and ended up crashing into the men's lavatories. She was, after all, of the generation who believed in absolute discretion. Yet this covered a multitude of outrageous escapades, at Bletchley and elsewhere. Jean Campbell-Harris, as she then was, had the force of a typhoon.

Born in 1922 to an American mother and a father in the Bengal Lancers, she entered a life of London luxury, in a grand house, surrounded by servants; her parents moved in the same social circles as the Prince of Wales. But the Wall Street Crash brought financial precarity to the family; and in any case the young Campbell Harris was already determined to outmanoeuvre convention. She attended a variety of boarding schools with little interest apart from acquiring a sharp talent for bridge. And she never had any airs: having left school at 15, she worked at the posh department store Peter Jones and as a farmhand on Lloyd George's estate.

For some young recruits to Bletchley, the institution reminded them a little of university. For Jean Campbell-Harris, there was surely something of the raucous boarding school too: as well as laundry baskets, she was noted for her energetic renditions of 'Chattanooga Choo Choo'. What she craved was dancing: along with her friends Sarah Norton and Osla Benning, she delighted in haring back to London. 'We danced all night and then went back,' she recalled. 'I took my chances with men at dances. There was a feeling of "live for the moment."' Like many at Bletchley, she also found vigorous outdoor exercise a release. 'Winston Churchill gave us two tennis courts,' she remembered.

She maintained a certain discretion about the finer details of her codebreaking days, but occasionally she would be moved to comment on the way it was depicted in popular culture. 'I think the acting is absolutely superb,' Baroness Trumpington said of *The Imitation Game*, which starred Benedict Cumberbatch as Alan Turing and Keira Knightley as his mathematician fiancée Joan Clarke. 'The chap who plays Turing is fantastic. I really do think his girlfriend is too. If only she had been as ravishingly pretty as the one in the film was . . . I only met the famous and wonderful Turing once,' she went on, 'when I was asked to take a piece of paper to him. I think I just said: "Here is that piece of paper that you need."'

Her post-war life was uproariously event-filled, taking in Paris, New York, being at Cliveden with Stephen Ward and on board Concorde for its maiden flight, and elevation to the peerage in 1980. Bletchley Park could not have asked for a finer and less conventional ambassador.

Gordon Welchman

A great many people have worked for the estimable John Lewis Partnership across the years. Few, however, could have had as many secrets as this man. This was just after the war: Gordon Welchman was Director of Research, and his focus was new technology and its potential applications.

His time at John Lewis was brief: Welchman, himself Never Knowing Undersold, yearned for the wider horizons of the United States. Throughout the 1950s, he blazed a trail at the renowned Massachusetts Institute of Technology, drawing on some very specialised and advanced computer knowledge. His expertise was also sought by the US's National Security Agency: not an accolade bestowed upon many British academics. Yet this brilliant career came juddering unjustly to an halt in the early 1980s when he wrote a book, telling the world precisely what he had done in the war.

For it was Gordon Welchman who, more than anyone else, transformed Bletchley Park from a cottage industry into a vast codebreaking factory, with branches in every corner of the world.

As well as intense mathematical and technical skills, this young mathematics don from Sidney Sussex College, Cambridge with the air of a 1930s matinee idol – natty tweeds, sports car, pencil moustache, a certain talent for skiing – that made him one of the few at Bletchley Park to cut a dash, brought something even more vital to the war effort: a gift for organisation.

It was also Welchman who teamed up with Alan Turing to bring the codebusting Bombe machines into play. He gave the design an extra feature known as the 'diagonal board', which had the effect of cutting through some millions more potential combinations. In addition to all of this, he headed up Hut 6, drawing in encryptions from the German army and air efforts and becoming in effect the beating heart of Bletchley's war.

Welchman was not unduly afflicted by modesty, and why should he have been? He was prominent in the line-up on the day in spring 1941 when Winston Churchill paid the top-secret site a discreet visit. The Park's director Edward Travis had instructed his colleagues that they should limit their exchanges with the PM to just a few well-chosen words. But to Travis's evident disapproval Welchman managed to draw Churchill into some banter. He remembered later that the Prime Minister turned to him and gave him 'a grand schoolboy wink'.

But Welchman was also, perhaps on account of his own relative youth, attuned to what a curiously romantic place Bletchley Park could be. One summer's evening, he recalled, he was walking the towpath of the nearby Grand Union Canal at sunset when suddenly, as though hearing ghosts from centuries past, the air was filled with the sound of a perfectly sung madrigal. Rounding a bend, he came upon a group of young codebreakers sitting on the bank, under the crimson sky, singing perfect *a capella*.

By 1943, Welchman was setting sail across the Atlantic – like Turing, a vital codebreaking emissary – and it was here that his long relationship with America began. After the war, Welchman maintained his close links with the US intelligence community, and when, in the 1970s, the first real disclosures were made about Bletchley Park and its wartime role, he clearly felt it was time he helped set the historical record straight.

In 1982, his book *Inside Hut 6* was published. Mrs Thatcher's government, in tandem with GCHQ, reacted with discomfort and some anger. That such a senior figure within that secret realm could have thrown so much of what was still classed as Official Secrets into the light came as a shock. The furious reaction shocked Welchman to the same extent. An even greater shock came when the US authorities stripped him of his prized security clearance.

The punishment seemed disproportionate; the book was not an act of treason, but an effort to frame what would become a much-told story. Indeed, it is only in recent years that Gordon Welchman and his vast contribution to Bletchley's success have received proper recognition.

Denise St Aubyn Hubbard

Although an intense spirit of adventure was a leitmotif among Bletchley Park's female recruits, it was perhaps embodied most fully in a woman who later set a world record for sailing across the Atlantic single-handed. Denise St Aubyn Hubbard seemed born to live in water: as a youngster brought up in 1930s Egypt she had won prizes for high diving (one presented to her by King Faroukh). She had gone on to compete in the 1948 Olympics. A move to Chichester after she married introduced her to sailing, a pursuit that came to dominate her entire life. Curiously, her time at Bletchley Park, fascinating though it was, could not quite match the sheer mad colour of everything that went before or came after.

Born Denise Newman in London, 1924, she grew up in the Middle East as her father was working for one of the oil companies that would go on to make the region so geopolitically vital. The Cairo of her childhood was still in thrall to the spirit of empire: lazy ceiling fans, opulent hotels, buzzing souks. War brought the family back to England, and Denise Newman volunteered for the Air Ministry. It soon became apparent she was fluent in Arabic and French, and such talent could not be wasted. Soon she found herself immersed in Bletchley's intensive Japanese language course, the essence of which she had mastered within six months. Then began her time working on the abstruse mysteries of Japanese cryptography.

Her life beyond this proceeded at the same extraordinary pace. While the austere 1948 Olympics – accommodation in cramped, shared rooms in the Domestic Science College in bomb-cratered Pimlico – was not especially happy, the life on the wave was to follow with gusto. When her marriage to Vyvyan St Aubyn Hubbard directly after the war broke down two decades later, she volunteered for the Royal Navy Auxiliary Service, and then set up her own sailing school. In 1988, a friend's offer of a yacht drew her into a transatlantic single-handed race. It was frequently a harrowing ordeal, with the navigation packing up, and sails falling into mighty waves. But she made it, at the age of 63. That laughing indefatigability must have made her a tremendous asset to the Bletchley team.

Queen, the, 85, 123, 137
Rattigan, Terence, 15
Reed, Henry, **100–101**
Rees, Professor David, **32–33**
Roberts, Jerry, **122–123**
Rock, Margaret, **192–193**
Roseveare, Robert, **215–216**
Rothschild, Dame Miriam, **126–127**
Russell, Anne, **176–177**
Sandars, Nancy, **154–155**
Scott-Thomas, Kristin, 169
Seligman, Nancy Joan, **220–221**
Spry, Constance, 22
Staveley, Stuart, **156–157**
Strachey, Lytton, 60, 184
Strachey, Oliver, **60–61**
Suter, Elizabeth, **19–20**
Taylor, Telford, **66–67**, 115
Thelwell, Norman, 21
Thesiger, Wilfred, 17
Thirsk, Joan, **161–162**
Thomas, Dylan, 98
Tiltman, Brigadier John, 60, 67, **194–196**
Townend, Brian, **213–214**
Travis, Sir Edward, 69, 121, 141, **180–181**, 209, 233

Tremain, Rose, 95
Trudeau, Justin, 226
Trumpington, Baroness (Jean Campbell Harris), **230–231**
Turing, Alan, 25, 26, 31, 37, 39, 40, 49, **76–77**, 91, 117, 128, 141, 149, 176, 182, 185, 201, 233
Tutte, Professor Bill, **41–42**
Twinn, Peter, 117, **128–129**, 193
Twitchett, Denis, **167–168**
Valentine, Jean, 19, **136–137**, 214, 240
Ward, Stephen, 231
Warhol, Andy, 243
Watkins, Vernon, **98–99**
Webb, Charlotte (Betty), **237–239**
Welchman, Gordon, 26, 32, 78, 86, 113, 128, 148, **232–234**, 215, 231
Williams, Lilian, **244–245**
Wilson, Angus, **94–95**
Wilson, Harold, 27
Wittgenstein, Ludwig, 76
Wylie, Shaun, **90–91**
Yoxall, Leslie, **78–79**

Index

Johnson, President Lyndon B., 72
Jones, Eric, 120–121
Karloff, Boris, 14
Kasparov, Gary, 46
Kelly, Grace, 16
Kennedy, President John F., 72
Keynes, John Maynard, 184
Kipling, Rudyard, 220
Knightley, Kiera, 182, 231
Knox, Alfred Dillwyn (Dilly), 83, 113, 128, 144, 183, **184–185**, 188, 192, 209, 212
Kubrick, Stanley, 36
Kullback, Solomon, **70–71**
Lawn, Oliver, 29, **84–85**, 138
Lawry, Beryl, **104–105**
Leavis, F. R., 102
Lee, Jennie, 149
Leigh Fermor, Patrick, 18
Lever, Mavis (later Batey), 83, **144–145**, 192, 193
Lynch, Arnold, **48–49**
Mackenzie, Sheila (later Lawn), 29, **138–139**
Macmillan, Harold, 17
MacNeice, Louis, 100
Maguire, Waldo, **174–175**
Malle, Louis, 242
Marks, Leo, 16
Maugham, W. Somerset, 22
McEwan, Ian, 95
Menzies, Sir Stewart, 181
Michie, Donald, **45–47**
Miliband, David, 202
Milner-Barry, **26–27**
Montefiore, Ruth Sebag, **204–205**
Mountbatten, Lord, 9
Murdoch, Rupert, 149
Murrill, Herbert, **58–59**
Newman, Professor Max, 33, 37, 39, 41, **39–40**, 123
Newton-John, Brinley, **56-57**
Newton-John, Olivia, 56, 57
Nixon, President Richard M., 191
Noskwith, Rolf, **200–201**
Oldfield, Bruce, 20
Ondaatje, Michael, 169
Parris, Matthew, 215
Pears, Peter, 54
Poore, Duncan, **130–131**
Prince Charles, 20, 21, 127
Prince Philip, 11, 12
Princess Anne, 20
Putt, S. Gorley, **102–103**
Quayle, Anthony, 13

Crankshaw, William Edward, 25, **172–173**
Cumberbatch, Benedict, 76, 231
Dacre, Lord (Hugh Trevor-Roper), **158–160**
Dalai Lama, 17
De Grey, Nigel, 141, **186–187**
de la Falaise, Comtesse Maxime, **242–243**
De Valois, Ninette, 151
Denniston, Alastair, 91, 180, **208–210**, 216, 225, 226
Diana Spencer, Lady, 20, 21
Egremont, the Dowager Lady, **17–18**
Eliot, T. S., 98
Ernst, Max, 243
Evans, Professor John, **163–164**
Eytan, Walter, **198–199**, 201
Fairlie, Professor Alison, **108–109**
Fawcett, Jane, **151–153**
Fiennes, Ralph, 169
Fleming, Ian, 24, 50, 80, 156, 157
Flowers, Tommy, **43–44**, 48, 49, 123
Formby, George, 14
Foss, Hugh, **28–29**, 138
Friedman, William, **68–69**
Gable, Clark, 127
Galilee, Mimi, **140–141**
Galitzine, Princess George, **15–16**
Getty, John Paul III, 242
Goldberg, Sidney, **202–203**
Golombek, Harry, **30–31**, 174
Good, Irving John (Jack), **36–38**
Harris, Robert, 27
Harrison, Edgar, **222–223**
Hayward, Gil, **50–51**
Heath, Edward, 191, 220, 221
Herivel, John, **86–87**, 218
Hess, Myra, 54
Hilton, Peter, **88–89**
Hinsley, Harry, **146–147**, 190
Howard, Jean, **169–170**
Hubbard, Denise St Aubyn, **235–236**
Hudson, Rosalind, **21–22**
Hyson, Dorothy, **13–14**, 141
James, Sid, 116
Jenkins, Lord (Roy) of Hillhead, 10, 123, **218–219**

Index

Acheson, Dean, 73
Alexander, Hugh, 21, 26, **24–25**, 37, 78
Almásy, Count László, 169
Ashbee, Felicity, **165–166**
Astor, Nancy, 8
Astor, William Waldorf, 8
Auden, W. H., 58
Babbage, Dennis, **112–113**
Balme, Maurice, **211–212**
Baring, Sarah (née Norton), **8–10**, 12, 29, 219, 231
Batey, Keith, **82–83**, 84, 144, 193
Beaton, Cecil, 9, 13, 15
Benning, (Margaret) Osla, **11–12**, 231
Bernard, James, **54–55**
Betjeman, John, 151
Birch, Frank, **116–117**, 227
Blacker, Carmen, **106–107**
Blunt, Anthony, 119
Bonsall, Arthur, **190–191**

Bourne, Ruth, **240–241**
Briggs, Asa, **148–150**
Britten, Benjamin, 55
Brooke-Rose, Christine, **96–97**
Brown, Patricia, **224–225**
Bundy, William, 27, **72–73**
Burgess, Guy, 173
Cairncross, John, **118–119**
Calvocoressi, Peter, **114–115**
Churchill, Winston, 3, 26, 185, 186, 223
Clark, Kenneth, 163
Clarke, Arthur C., 36
Clarke, Joan, **182–183**, 192, 193, 201
Clayton, Aileen, **134–135**
Cohen, Jonathan, **80–81**
Cole, George, 117
Cooper, Joshua, 141, **188–189**, 190
Cooper, Margaret, **226–227**
Craig, Douglas, **62–63**

Lilian Evans was posted to Hut 3, and was fascinated to be thrown into this world composed of all conceivable backgrounds; the more aristocratic women, she noticed, never seemed snobbish. Partly they were all bonded by the ferocious intensity of the work – she recalled on one night shift seeing a colleague literally collapse with nervous strain. She was mindful of all the dances and revues and classical concerts that the authorities were providing, but escapism was largely impossible.

That said, artistic expression, and the art of linguistics, was important to Lilian; after the war, she moved to London to work with a leather export firm, but spent her spare time attending classes at the City Literary Institute in Covent Garden. When she retired to North Wales she supported the croquet club and the local drama group. 'My indomitable aunt Lilian Williams . . . lived an ordinary life,' wrote her obituarist in the *Guardian* after her death at 92 – 'or so we believed until she was able to disclose her work at Bletchley Park'.

Lilian Williams

This was a generation that took secrecy seriously. After all, it was not just the recruits to Bletchley who remained button-lipped about what they did; throughout the war years, everyone in the services grew used to being discreet. Lilian Williams, who had been selected for the world of codebreaking after confessing her love of solving anagrams in newspaper cryptic crosswords, in some ways embodied that dutiful silence. Her own life afterwards remained quiet, though not without its own rewards and satisfactions. The fact of having worked at the Park was itself a proud achievement, but one she could never allow herself to share with her family.

She hailed from Aberystwyth in west Wales where she had been born, one of six siblings, in 1917. Given that her father had been made to leave school before he gained a secondary education, the academic successes of his children were a blessing. In 1936, Lilian Evans won a scholarship to University College London to read French and German. Somehow, she temporarily evaded the notice of the codebreaking talent spotters, and began her war working for the Welsh Board of Health back in Cardiff.

It dawned on her that the Foreign Office might be able to make some use of her ability with German. She was not wrong. But she was puzzled when she talked to the interview panel of offering these skills and they seemed more excited about her love of crosswords. It was only when she arrived at Bletchley Park, with no idea of what it was she was being sent to, that the penny dropped.

find a way of shutting out the pressure. The heavy responsibility, added to the long hours of hyper-focused attention and the tortuous night shifts, led to a period of mental ill-health, which manifested itself in curious outbreaks of kleptomania. It was clear to the Park authorities that she had to be relieved.

A position was found for her in the US, and it was there that she met her first husband Comte Alan de la Falaise. Now she became Maxime with an m, but it was a short marriage, and he was impecunious, so she had to find ingenious ways to be the family breadwinner for herself and their two children.

The post-war years gave her a fresh burst of freedom, and she was greatly sought after as a muse by fashion houses and artists and film directors alike. In the 1950s she married John McKendry, a senior figure at New York's Metropolitan Museum of Art. She also had a relationship with the artist Max Ernst, and found herself invited into Andy Warhol's 'Factory' milieu. In the 1970s she was persuaded to make an appearance in the Andy Warhol film *Blood For Dracula*.

In addition to all this, she became an expert in cookery and food history — many smart kitchens in Chelsea were adorned with her volume *Seven Centuries of English Cooking*, which contained an un-ironic recipe for hedgehog.

Comtesse Maxime de la Falaise

Maxime de la Falaise was a complete original who could not be compartmentalised in any way. From *haute* fashion muse to cookery writer to star of 1970s underground schlock art-house films, her entire life was an aesthetic statement. With her lovers ranging from the film director Louis Malle to John Paul Getty III, and homes from Paris to New York, her post-war years were the definition of boho style and chic. She moved in the artiest of French circles, wore the coolest clothes, had a spirit that roamed free, and yet was blessed with the unselfconscious eccentricity and eclecticism that made her quite a specific English type. The only shame was that her time at Bletchley Park was so miserable.

Maxine (with an n) Birley, born in 1922, was the daughter of the portrait artist Oswald Birley, and her brother Mark was to become the proprietor of the nightclub Annabels. Childhood was divided between Hampstead, Charleston Manor in Sussex (the garden designed by Vita Sackville-West) and St Tropez. But the stylish, burnished luxury of those inter-war years was not, for her, an unthinking paradise; at home there was tension and unhappiness between her parents.

Her impulse, at the start of the war, was to volunteer for the WAAF, which in time led to her being plucked away for work at Bletchley Park. But Maxine Birley was among those who could not

When apprised of the super-secret codebreaking world she had entered, Ruth Henry was magnificently unimpressed. 'Having read books about Biggles and spies, I was aware that people were breaking each other's codes,' she remembered. However, there was a sense of dawning awe when she understood just how complex these codes were.

She did not spend long in Buckinghamshire. Instead, she was bound for the outstation at Eastcote in north-west London, which was filled with Bombes, each machine assigned to a different country or territory. The hours were grim, the strip lights mercilessly bright and 'green-tinged', the food 'appalling'. And yet there were bright sides. Eastcote was on the London Underground Piccadilly Line, which ran through to the West End. On rare free nights, Ruth enjoyed dancing and theatre.

After the war she learned shorthand, became a skilled typist, and stayed on with the Royal Navy and Port of London Authority for a short time. Marriage (she met her husband to be in 1946) brought a move to what was then the rather rough neighbourhood of Notting Hill, and thereafter to gentler Barnet, with the launderette business established in Temple Fortune.

For a great many people facing austerity after the war, practicality was a tremendous virtue. When the Bletchley secret was revealed in the 1970s, Ruth Bourne's RAF veteran husband showed a brief glimmer of abstracted interest. More rewarding in other ways were the years when she returned to the restored Park as an expert and much sought-after guide. She was to become one of Bletchley Park's best-known faces.

Ruth Bourne

The connection between breaking German codes and running a launderette in a genteel North London suburb might not seem immediately obvious. But for Ruth Bourne there was an obvious and practical link. As a Wren, she had spent three years wrangling with the vast (and temperamental) Bombe machines, their drums rotating, their rear wiring forever needing adjusting; in the years after the war, she and her husband, who was demobbed from the RAF, looked after bulky machines which also had endlessly rotating drums (business was brisk in the days before widespread domestic washing machines). Whereas others ascribed a near-mystical quality to the codebreaking life – its intense hermeticism, the transcendent intellects required to plunge deep into mathematical perplexities – Ruth Bourne (née Henry) approached it with a no-nonsense practicality.

Her talent was for languages. Born in 1926, she shone at her Birmingham school in the field of linguistics, gaining what was termed a 'matric' in French, Spanish and German. It earned her an open place at University College London. But by then Britain was midway through the war with Germany and, aged 17, Ruth Henry knew she had to contribute in whatever way the authorities saw best. She volunteered for the Wrens; was sent on the same naval training course to Tullichewan Castle in Scotland that Jean Valentine and others undertook; found herself being drawn aside from the other young women to be told that she was assigned to 'Special Duties X', and then sent south to Bletchley.

experiences. Not that long ago, Betty Webb featured on the cover of *National Geographic* magazine, and at the age of 98 was awarded France's highest civilian honour, the Legion d'honneur. Her younger self at Bletchley would have been speechless.

Because her position was secretarial and administrative to begin with, she was among the few who actually worked in the mansion itself, recalling ruefully how, on long winter night shifts, the warm flames from the coal fire would gradually die in the fireplace and a frosty chill would settle on the office. She became acquainted with all the intricacies of the decrypt operation while wrestling with the demands of the ATS, including endless gas mask drills.

To then be dispatched to Washington DC was a mark of her adaptability and also her trustworthiness; her role was to help with the Japanese code-cracking operation. Her work there continued as war in Europe ended in May 1945, and she remembered vividly the extraordinary atmosphere in Washington in August when it was announced that Japan had surrendered: there was a cacophony of car horns throughout the city. Then there were more details of the atomic bombs that had been detonated over Hiroshima and Nagasaki, and she recalled how the reality of the horror that had been perpetrated to end the war chilled her own joy.

Nor was her own life free from hazard. Having spent months trying to get passage back to England, all priority being given to servicemen in all corners of the world, she eventually managed to get a place on a troop ship, which then had painfully – and frighteningly – to navigate its way through the still mine-infested waters of the Atlantic.

Post-war life brought silence, secrecy, but also Shropshire tranquility. In 1975, upon publication of the first book to lift the lid on Bletchley, she was in Birmingham when by chance she walked past someone she fleetingly recognised from Bletchley. That woman recognised her too, and exclaimed: 'We can talk about it now!' But they never exchanged names and never saw each other again. And the habit of secrecy was ingrained: talk to whom, and why?

Happily, with the restoration of the Park came a sense that it was important for all veterans to relate their hitherto classified

Charlotte 'Betty' Webb

Regardless of whether Prime Minister Boris Johnson regards the phrase 'Special Relationship' – applied to Britain and America – as 'weak and needy', there were among the codebreakers those who took intense pride and pleasure at the unprecedented intelligence sharing with the US that developed during the war. And just as some American codebreakers came to the UK and smiled wryly when everything really did stop for tea, so the British personnel sent over to the US revelled in the reality of a land they had seen only on cinema screens.

Among the Bletchley-ites to make the journey was a young woman steeped in German language and culture called Charlotte Webb (known as 'Betty'). She travelled into the very heart of the US military establishment, working in the Pentagon. That she later came back to the UK to work in a quiet Shropshire school spoke of a life where discretion and duty were foremost.

She had been born in Shropshire in 1923, and her family had a military background. In the late 1930s, she spent time in Germany as an exchange student, and became quite close to the family she was billeted with. The distantly booming drums of war disturbed them all greatly, and when she left them she felt a wrench. Back in Britain as war came, she volunteered for the ATS – her home in Shropshire was far from the Luftwaffe's industrial targets, but she recalled seeing the darkness of the night sky illuminated by the bombing of Birmingham some 50 miles distant. Her ease with the German language put her on the radar for Bletchley.